I0199597

Applied Christianity:

Worldview Training for the 21st Century Christian

Applied Christianity:
Worldview Training for the 21st Century Christian
By Brian Horvath

ISBN: 978-0-578-68309-6

Praise for Mr. Horvath's Applied Christianity class

Growing up in a Christian family and going to Christian schools my whole life, it was easy for me to talk to Christian talk without living the Christian walk. It wasn't until I took Applied Christianity when I was motivated by Horvath to truly live out God's teachings and commands. It's one thing to be a passive consumer when it comes to church life, but it is a wonderful blessing when you start to become an active participant in God's plan. Horvath encouraged me to pursue God in all aspects of life.

—Kelsey Streicher (Mather), Class of 2014

Mr. Horvath's Applied Christianity challenged each and every one of us to 'choose differently' and to make sure everything we did, we 'did it right'. Although this may seem like a simple concept, each dare had its own package deal. You can't 'choose differently' without having your MEPS in order and you can't 'do it right' without changing how you think. Mr. Horvath pushed me beyond my comfort zone and because of that, Applied Christianity changed my entire life.

—Alaina Capoccia, Class of 2019

After surrendering myself to all I learned in Applied, which humbled me beyond explanation, and taking the blinders off (2 Corinthians 4:4) to dive into the Gospel on my own, I found my identity in the Cross of Christ. Applied Christianity changed my life, helping me to know the Truth of God's Word and how to store it in my heart (Psalm 119:11).

—Ross Lipari, Class of 2015

Applied Christianity gave me answers to questions I didn't even know I wanted to ask or even think about. It gave me a way to handle the outside world while holding true to my values and beliefs, and not BE shaken. The way we live the life GOD wants us to live has meaning behind it. Applied helped explain God's purpose for his creation; for me. I couldn't be more thankful for my experience.

—Julianne Weir, 2014

Applied Christianity allows each person to examine their worldview and search for consistency. For Christians, that is found in the Bible. God's truth is further revealed and applied by relating scripture to present day topics and issues. Applied's content is crucial to the present-day Christian; and the experience is eye-opening, as the world's deceptive philosophy takes a backseat to Christ's unadulterated Word.

—Alec Escandon, Class of 2019

Our faith walk is a continuous learning process. On this journey, we must learn to live out an active faith, to hold ourselves accountable for our actions and decisions, and to surround ourselves with Christ-centered people. Applied Christianity teaches how to do exactly that, and much more.

—Tyler Prisby, Class of 2016

Dedication

To AJ and Chi, that you may always start and stay at the cross.

Special Thanks

Anthony Horvath and Reilley "Fav" Warner for taking the time to edit and read, *Applied Christianity*

Sincere appreciation to Jacquelyn Schwark for providing *Applied Christianity's* foreword.

To those who have influenced and made a difference in the life entrusted to me by the Lord, thank you. Your friendship and fellowship are appreciated.

And of course, thank you to Kara, the wife entrusted to me by the Lord, for her continued support and encouragement.

Table of Contents

Foreword

I am a unique child of God, full of potential, and washed in the blood of Christ. *This* is my identity. With the guidance of Brian Horvath and Applied Christianity, I have grown to recognize who I am and whose I am. Regardless of the labels the world uses to define me, in Christ I know that I am a daughter of the king. To this day, when asked, "Who are you?" the answer is simple: I am a unique child of God, full of potential, and washed in the blood of Christ.

However, my answer to this question was not always this clear. For a long time, I struggled with various futile attempts to define my identity with worldly accomplishments. I looked to my achievements in the classroom and my success on the basketball court to give my life meaning and purpose. When I arrived in Brian Horvath's senior theology class called Applied Christianity, I was unsure of exactly who I was and where I was heading next.

Similar to many others, as a senior in high school I wrestled with where my next steps would take me. The uncertainty of my future had me desperately seeking direction. I wanted worldly advice, someone to tell me where to go to school and what I should study. Mr. Horvath did not oblige; instead, his advice was simple. He redirected me to the foot of the cross. As I struggled to make difficult decisions about my earthly future, he helped to broaden my perspective by assuring me that as long as I loved God, loved others, and shared the gospel, it wouldn't matter where I went to school or what I decided to study.

Despite initially wanting nothing to do with being an educator, Horvath saw my potential as a leader and patiently guided me in that direction. Today, as a current teacher and coach, I am forever thankful for the role he played in helping me discern my calling. Every day, I am presented with opportunities to positively impact children. As he would say, "Another day, another opportunity." This is one of the many valuable lessons I learned from Horvath in Applied Christianity. Each child I reach directly ties back to the immeasurable impact that he had on me. Throughout his years of teaching, Brian Horvath has touched hundreds of lives. All of those students are now out in the world creating more disciples. I believe his impact on the world via this ripple effect is far greater than you or I can imagine.

This book will only magnify that ripple effect. *Applied Christianity* will equip you to "give an answer to everyone who asks you to give the reason for the hope that you have." (1 Peter 3:15). What will happen when your faith gets called into question? How will you respond when your worldview doesn't align with your friend's, professor's, or family's worldview? Are you prepared to defend the gospel? Horvath walks you through life's big questions and encourages you to think critically about how you will answer them. Prepare to be challenged to evaluate your perspective as you journey through this book. *Applied Christianity* calls readers to action by challenging them to confidently discern what they believe and why they believe it. The tough questions and valuable insights Brian Horvath provides in *Applied Christianity* make it a must-read for every 21st century Christian.

Beloved child of God,
Jacquelyn Schwark, Class of 2013

Preface

It was around my sophomore year of college when I finally decided on a career that seemed interesting. Like many college students, my major changed as frequently as Michigan's weather. Social work lasted a week before changing to pastor ministry. Months after realizing pastoral ministry was not the right choice, I hesitantly chose education. Academics were not my forte. Anyone familiar with my lack of academic success growing up would have laughed at the decision, "Horvath, a teacher? Right."

I was confident the classroom was a good place to land, and even more confident that teaching mathematics, history, science, or literature would have been a disservice to any high school student. My intended goal was to teach theology at a Lutheran high school. Problem was, secular states did not issue teaching licenses for theology (separation of church and state). Normally, if you wanted to teach theology, you majored in a state certifiable content area (math, science, etc.). If you were fortunate enough, the hiring school would need a section or two of theology covered on top of the state certifiable content area that aligned with your major.

You would teach history and Old Testament, or biology and Christian ethics—but again, only if the school had theology classes available. You may end up teaching six sections of biology and no theology. Problematic if your only goal was teaching theology.

Knowing it was risky, I settled on majoring in theology and minoring in education. Rolling the dice, I was hoping a school would have a need for a full-time theology teacher at the exact time I was graduating Concordia University Wisconsin. God closed all possible doors. There was a youth director position available in Florida, but that interview bore no fruit. Debt and degree in hand, and without employment, my wife and I headed to Missouri where I attended Concordia Seminary, St. Louis, earning a two-year, Master of Arts in Religion degree (MAR). As my time at Concordia ended, emails were sent to Lutheran high schools in the Detroit area seeking an opportunity.

One school responded: Lutheran North in Macomb, Michigan. Historical and systematic theology were my majors at the seminary. Lutheran North wanted me to teach practical theology. Despite my education to that point, this was something I didn't know much about.

That did not matter of course, and acceptance of the offer quickly followed. Practical theology for the win. Without a teaching license and without hesitation, I accepted the call to teach 12th grade theology. Essentially, it was going to be my responsibility to prepare the graduating seniors for the rest of their lives. Easy day. Complicating matters, like many Lutheran high schools across the nation, Lutheran North lacked a tried and true theology curriculum. Both a blessing and a curse. I would be starting from scratch. Fortunately, I can adapt and improvise as needed, which is a necessity in a society that changes rapidly despite God's Truth standing the test of time.

To communicate His truth, I would focus on building relationships with students while using the Socratic Method as my primary means of challenging the young men and women to consider who they are, what they believe in, why they believe what they believe, and what their belief looks like manifested in every aspect of the life entrusted to them by God. Every day since then has been seen as an opportunity to dare students to take ownership of their faith.

Simplified the curriculum focuses on three areas: Christian Apologetics, Christian Ethics and Christian Sanctification. Admittedly, Living the Faith's[1] early years focused more on teaching content than anything else. Like many new teachers, I spent most of my time in survival mode. Focus changed from teaching content to developing young men and women within that content.

Not only would questions about God's existence be answered, but we would also consider some other practical issues such as sex, drugs, tattoos, friendships, dating and everything between, seeking to show how one's faith can be applied in our daily lives. Major ethical issues such as homosexuality, abortion and euthanasia would be covered. We would discuss student mental and emotional health and how those areas would be impacted as during their transition from high school to college (and beyond). Mind, body, and soul would be addressed because the whole person was about to leave the safe confines of high school and enter the big bad "real world."

Safe to say, I see myself as not only a teacher, but also as a guide, life coach, brother, and father. I stopped teaching content only and started teaching *life* within the content. Many former students have communicated their appreciation of Applied. Speaking with great humility, student and parent appreciation has increased from one year to the next. Alumni have repeatedly expressed desire to retake senior theology as perspectives on life change quickly after graduation. Handfuls of parents have expressed an interest in sitting in Applied

[1] Applied used to be called Living the Faith.

hoping to learn what their children learned. Humbling to say the least.

Applied Christianity is the opportunity alumni and parents have long desired.

(Saving the reader confusion, when discussing the class itself, I refer to it as Applied. When referring to the book, the phrase *Applied Christianity* is used.)

First day of school
"Dare You to Move," by Switchfoot

Three months have gone by without students being dictated by a bell system. Once that first 7:50am bell rings, a collective groan can be heard throughout the hallway. I smile. Two and half months off was needed and appreciated, but new students present new opportunities. Five minutes later, 7:55am, a second bell rings, indicating the beginning of their senior year. Before the bell finishes its second ring, I push 'play' on the media player. Switchfoot's "Dare You to Move" begins.

Instead of opening their senior year discussing the syllabus, I have chosen to challenge seniors to take ownership of the faith they profess. Switchfoot's, "Dare You to Move" is my chosen vehicle.

Listening to the song, students are expected to highlight lyrics applicable to their lives. Those lyrics will be the basis for our conversation which I hope catches their attention and gets them excited for the school year and their faith. Readers of *Applied Christianity* are encouraged to read or listen to "Dare You to Move" before moving through the rest of the book. Important lines that stand out and are discussed in class are:

Welcome to the planet, welcome to existence
Everybody's watching you now
I dare you to move like today never happened before
The tension is here between who you are and who you could be
Maybe forgiveness is right where you fell
I dare you to move

Seniors are expected to offer their own insights, but their comments prompt me to share my own, as well. Switchfoot welcomes their listeners to the planet and to existence. Applied's classroom is filled with reminders that the alternative to existence is non-existence. Every day is a gift, an opportunity given by the Lord. What will we do with that gift and opportunity? For better or worse, everyone is watching, waiting to see how we cash in God's gift of life.

Instead of taking life for granted, embrace the day, and live today like today never happened before. Imagine today was the first day you had ever seen a crystal blue sky, radiant flowers, bright green trees swaying in the wind. Imagine it is the first day you have ever seen your parents, siblings, or even teachers. Such a perspective allows for a freshness often dulled by life's unpleasant routines. Tension rises between embracing the moment and being sucked down by the prospect of 179 more school days.

One student's comment: "Maybe this is the year that I take my faith seriously. A fresh start."

The tension between who we are and who we could be in Christ is real. Sin pulls us away from the potential God has given us to live His purpose. But, if you are willing to recognize God's forgiveness is right where you fell, there is no reason to dwell in the past or be weighed down by the tension. Today is another day and another opportunity to be who God has called you to be—a unique child of God, full of potential, washed in the blood of Christ.

I dare you to embrace the opportunity, walk in His truth, and lead others to His love.

I dare you.

Introduction

Looking back at my first few years of teaching, I feel bad for Applied's initial classes. As stated earlier, I was starting Applied's curriculum from scratch. I knew that Lee Strobel's *The Case for Christ* was going to be a centerpiece even if I did not know how. Lacking knowledge and experience, I decided I would make worksheets for every chapter. Each chapter contained at least twenty questions that needed to be answered. Students were given two class periods (give or take) to read the chapter and answer questions. Yikes. Pedagogical embarrassment. Furthermore, high school seniors were asked to independently read and work for entire class periods. Classroom management nightmare.

This was the method for the first few years of teaching as I tried to avoid being duct taped to a wall or punched. In between apologetics, we still discussed sanctification and major ethical issues. Dating, relationships, marriage, homosexuality, and the death penalty were all conversations needing to be discussed. Exactly when and where in the curriculum these conversations would take place was figured out on the fly. I learned that an entire semester of two-page handouts and classical apologetics, followed by a semester of ethics was unpleasant for both student and teacher.

Initially, that was the curriculum: apologetics followed by ethics. As years progressed, content was broken up with connections being made across apologetics, ethics, and sanctification. Today, Applied's curriculum begins by providing common arguments for God's existence which naturally proceeds into worldview investigation, which naturally leads into worldview application.

Remember, the major purpose of Applied is to challenge students to contemplate *what* they believe in, *why* they believe in what they believe, and then, what does their belief *look like* when manifested? Starting with God's existence makes sense: start at the beginning because "*finis origine pendet.*"[2]

A belief or lack of belief in God influences one's worldview. It determines your starting perspective. If God is responsible for life, and life carries God's image, then we want to know how that perspective influences racism, abortion, and dating (as examples). For example, Genesis 1:26-27 applies to racism, abortion, and dating (and many other areas):

---

[2] Latin for, "the end depends upon the beginning."

Then God said, “Let us make mankind in our image, in our likeness, so that they may rule over the fish in the sea and the birds in the sky, over the livestock and all the wild animals, and over all the creatures that move along the ground.” So, God created mankind in His own image, in the image of God he created them; male and female he created them.

Students are challenged to follow their worldview to its logical conclusion. How does one’s monotheistic worldview influence ethical issues?

God’s existence——-My worldview——-influences IVF…
God’s existence——-My worldview——-influences abortion…
God’s existence——-My worldview——-influences euthanasia…
God’s existence——-My worldview——-influences stem cell research…

Examining God’s existence and one’s worldview fills first quarter with life’s most challenging questions. Second quarter begins by applying their worldview to sanctity of life issues but concludes with historical apologetics. The change is needed as the first few months of school can be emotionally, mentally, and spiritually intense. Historical apologetics changes the mood and focus of Applied. Common questions and accusations against Christianity are addressed:

When were the Gospels written?
Where the Gospels written by eyewitnesses?
If two of the Gospels were not written by eyewitnesses, then who wrote them?
Can we trust their authorship?
What makes us think the names attached to the authors are correct?

Incoming students carry erroneous assumptions that must be addressed. Historical apologetics is not always as entertaining as the students would like, but the Scriptures are the Christian’s source of Truth. Failure to trust in the Scriptures leads to their immediate dismissal by the students. As dry as the content may be for some, most of the students understand the importance of addressing these historical questions.

Applied’s first semester progression looks like this:

God's existence—my worldview—life issues—historical apologetics

After a few weeks of discussing whether we can trust certain aspects of Scripture, we apply our trust to Biblical topics such as marriage, dating, tattoos, and friendships. Second semester begins with an intense introspection of daily influences.

The rest of the school year shifts back and forth between apologetics, ethics, and sanctification. I am proud to say, that with how the content is delivered, our conversations on ethics and sanctification have an apologetical feel. Never once do we abandon the early foundational work discussed first semester. At all times, we contrast the secular worldview to the Christian worldview. Continuous connections and transitions are evident from one topic to the next. If you are a Christian, *this* is what life looks like in every possible area. Whether the student is an atheist, or a theist matters not. We begin with the earliest question possible, God's existence.

God doesn't exist——my worldview——influences life how…

To some students' disappointment, I do not engage in hostile arguments with those who disagree with class content (Christian or non-Christian). Most individuals, Christians, and non-Christians do not know why they believe what they believe. Education is freely provided to the atheist, theist, and agnostic. One can rest assure that students of Applied or Lutheran North, have not been "brainwashed." Both the Christian worldview and the secular, atheistic worldview are represented. Lutheran North is a Christian school and thus the Christian perspective is presented while the atheistic worldview is described, with gentleness and respect, to be incorrect and incoherent.

Applied Christianity (this book) contains six parts which does not reflect the true order of Applied (the class). During the school year, we bob and weave between apologetics, ethics, and sanctification. *Applied Christianity* combines first semester historical apologetics with second semester historical apologetics to save the reader confusion.

Part six contains insights on popular videos shown throughout the school year. Applied students will recall that their first day began listening to Switchfoot's, "Dare You to Move." Including personal commentary on the song in *Applied Christianity's* unit on God's existence did not make much sense. The opening activities that begin each class period carry significant implications for the students and are staples of Applied's curriculum and worthy of inclusion in *Applied Christianity*.

Understand that Applied covers a lot of content which is distributed across one-hundred and eighty school days. One could easily spend an entire year only discussing God's existence, marriage and sexuality, or the historicity of the New Testament. Please do not expect this book to be the end all, be all, of scholarship on every specific topic covered in the world. *Applied Christianity* is an explanation of what is discussed over the course of the year in Applied. Not every detail is included and not every question asked in class is presented. Nor is every scholar quoted or recent book cited. Even one-hundred and eighty school days is not enough to discuss every insight on every topic.

Now, hurry up and do not be tardy. Be sure to have your desk cleared, except for your writing utensil and notebook.

Part I

God's Existence

Chapter 1

God's Existence: Cosmological Argument

Applied's first weeks create a foundation used the rest of the academic year and beyond. Applied's first days provide a series of dares and inspirations for each student.

Periods begin with three or four impactful applicable music videos.[3] Daily routines established at the beginning of class make it abundantly clear how Applied's classroom management will operate the next ten months. Class begins at the bell, or earlier.

Following an exhilarating soliloquy of the syllabus, Applied's second week begins with an explanation of my path into the classroom. This is an eye-opening experience for students who, for reasons unknown to me, walk into Applied Christianity assuming my life has been perfect. Five minutes later, students realize their assumptions are wrong. At the end, I assure intimidated students that I am not there to walk over them, but to walk with them in their faith journey.[4] Laying these foundational bricks and routines are significant for the rest of the school year, and unbeknownst to them, the rest of their lives.[5] How does one successfully navigate life if their foundation is weak or non-existent? Our first foundational brick laid, and unit of content covered, are common arguments and proofs for God's Existence.

Conversations on godly living or a theistic approach to ethical issues are difficult if one is unsure of God's existence. So, in Applied, five classic arguments for God's existence are introduced.

1. Cosmological Argument
2. Teleological Argument
3. Ontological Argument
4. Moral Law Argument
5. The Empty Tomb Argument

The day's anticipatory set requires students to be partnered up and provided a handful of toothpicks. Their first set of instructions are simple: Relate these toothpicks to God's existence. Student responses are consistent year after year:

---

[3] "Dare You to Move" by Switchfoot is played on the first day and last day of school.

[4] The syllabus is intense as I challenge students with Socrates's words, "the unexamined life is one not worth living," but also Applied is not snack time or recess.

[5] Starting class immediately at the bell, not talking out of turn and desks being on the dots in straight lines are not Napoleonic commands. They provide order, structure and discipline which are essential ingredients to living a systematic theology.

1. A toothpick picks food out of my teeth like God picks sin out of my life.
2. Toothpicks hold sandwiches together like God holds our lives together.
3. God is pointy on both sides like a toothpick.
4. There are many toothpicks but there is one God.

After a few minutes of confused conversation, we adapt the prompt: Relate the toothpicks to the *argument* for God's existence. Students are confused even more. Many students return to their initial answers about sin and God holding our lives together. A few students begin moving in the desired direction but lack a follow-through explanation. Most of the time, students create pictures or spell words on their desks, prompting an instructor's comment on their creativity, "John's on the right track." I say it loud enough for the entire classroom to hear. John is clueless, and so too are the rest of the students. Priceless.

Hoping to provide clarity and direction towards the end goal, a third prompt is provided: Using the toothpicks, *prove* God's existence. After a quick best two out of three series of Rock-Paper-Scissors, the winner chooses whether they will pretend to be a Christian or an atheist for this role-playing discussion. Most of Lutheran North's students possess a Christian worldview, thus placing them in the majority. This position of comfort changes once they attend their secular universities and find themselves in the minority. Knowing how to communicate one's faith to a non-believer becomes essential as their worldview will be directly and indirectly challenged after graduation. Role-playing between the two different worldviews is common practice in Applied for said reason. Using the toothpicks, the Christian (whether they are a Christian or not) needs to prove God's existence to the atheist (whether they are an atheist or not).

Conversations are heading in the right direction and class ends just as students are beginning to find a possible solution to the day's puzzle. Students are left hanging until the next day where an impactful video awaits their return.[6] Perfect timing.

The following day, the "circle of death" is introduced. Uncomfortable (feeling like death for some) as it is for students to have the entire class looking at them, being placed on the spot better prepares students for a lifetime of future conversations with non-believers, spouses, and CEOs. Within the larger "circle of death" are two desks facing each other waiting for students who will amaze the class with a

---

[6] "Meant to Live," by Switchfoot

solution to the challenge of proving God's existence with merely a toothpick. In one desk sits a student pretending to be an atheist while the other desk houses a Christian. We laugh, stare, cringe, and sometimes scratch our heads in confusion. Every now and then though, a few students will enlighten their classmates:

Christian: What is this?
Atheist: A toothpick
Christian: Where did the toothpick come from?
Atheist: People in a factory made it
Christian: Where did those people come from?
Atheist: Their parents…
Christian: And where did their parents come from?
Atheist: Um, their parents?
Christian: And their parents?
Atheist: The Big Bang.
Christian: And where precisely did that come from?
Atheist: Gas, particles, matter, etc.
Christian: And where did the material from for the Big Bang come from?
Atheist: I don't know.
Christian: Exactly… (further explanation follows)

The student's brief explanation that *something* had to cause everything else into existence introduces the cosmological argument for God's existence. It is possible that the individuals in the circle of death may be atheists or agnostic. Eternal salvation of each student is always on my mind, but I am not interested in beliefs at this point. I want the students entrusted to me by God to all be Christians. Right now, though, they are simply being provided an education on the prevailing arguments used across the world for God's existence.[7] Ignorance is not a place to dwell within, nor a place students are kept. If you are going to be an atheist or Christian, at least know why.

Something had to start *everything.* Predictably, seeing the direction the argument is heading, an inquisitive student raises their hand asking a fair question, "Then where did God come from?"

I start my response by providing students the definition and framework of a syllogism, which is a line of logical reasoning that contains multiple premises that lead into a logical (or illogical)

---

[7] Arguments that are used against Christians and arguments that will be discussed in collegiate philosophy classes.

conclusion. Borrowing (legally) and modifying slightly from Carm.org:[8]

Premise 1: Things exist
Premise 2: It is possible for those things to not exist
Premise 3: If it has the possibility of not existing, but does exist, it has been caused into existence by something else
Premise 4: There cannot be an infinite number of causes to bring something into existence
An infinite regression of causes ultimately has no initial cause, which means there is no cause of existence
Since the universe exist, it must have a cause

Conclusion 1: Therefore, there must be an uncaused cause of all things
Conclusion 2: The uncaused cause must be God

Big words may make it seem complicated, but it is simple: The book you are currently reading could not have created itself. To create itself, it would first have to exist. That is illogical and impossible. Something had to make the book. An author, perhaps. But where did the author come from? From his parents, of course. And where did they come from? Their parents. And where did those parents come from? Their parents.

This regression or moving backwards between sets of parents that created each other cannot go on forever (infinitely). How did the first set of parents come into existence? There had to be an initial cause to the progression of finite parents. Something, or someone in this case, that caused the first set of parents that caused the existence of the rest of the parents.

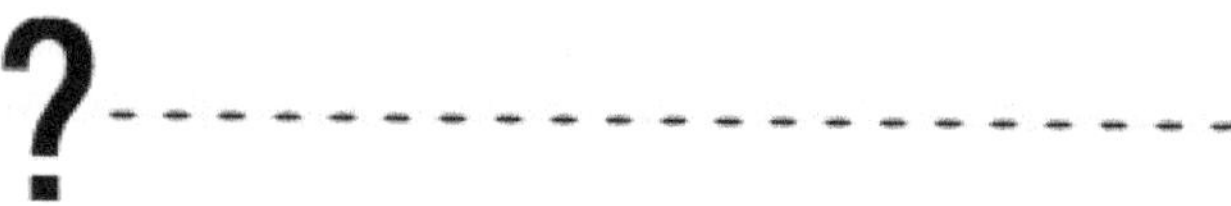

Continuing our line of reasoning, the universe also had a beginning. And if the universe had a beginning, it too was brought into existence. But, because the universe like the book cannot bring itself into

[8] Christian Apologetics & Research Ministry is a prominent voice in Internet apologetics. A 'must have' resource in your favorites list.

existence out of nothing, it too had a cause.

Christians reason that because there cannot be an infinite regression of causes of causes of causes, etc. there must have been a first Uncaused Cause of all things that started everything else: God.

Back to our question, "Where did God come from?" Your typical and appropriate statement of faith is that God always has been and always will be. This will not satisfy the atheist nor the questioning Christian but adding a word to the syllogism above assists in addressing the question: finite.

Premise 1: Finite things exist
Premise 2: Finite things cannot bring themselves into existence

The syllogism continues with its logical line of reasoning.

God is not finite. Everyone admits a book is limited by time and space. It cannot have created itself. To do so, it would first have to exist. It is finite. Honest philosophers or questioners will recognize that anytime the Christian God is being discussed, we mean the God that is outside of time and space. He is eternal and always has been. Unlike the universe, God is not limited by time and space. He created time and space and resides outside of each.

If God were limited by time and space or was not eternal, He would not be God. "You mean to tell me, that you have faith that God always has been and always will be?" asks the skeptic.

Here the Christian readily acknowledges the dreaded f-word: Faith. Believing in God's eternity is based on "blind" faith. God's existence and eternity outside of time and space cannot be empirically proven. If I could can snap my fingers and make God appear, that might be impressive. Though, any God that would be subject to the flippant snapping of fingers would not be an impressive deity.

What about atheists though? Do they also extend "blind" faith? Atheists may argue tooth and nail they do not rely on the f-word because they are above such blind statements of faith. They would never subject themselves to such idiocy as believing in God.[9] To believe God exists, let alone created the universe out of nothing, would to them be intellectual suicide. Yet, atheists find themselves in the same position as the Christian regarding the origins of the universe. What preceded the Big Bang? Nothing? Emptiness? Space? Other universes?

---

[9] The Internet is loaded with examples of atheists accusing Christians of relying on blind faith and being ignorant fools. Search at your heart's contempt for examples.

What caused those universes into existence? Unanswered and unanswerable questions begin to add up. Atheist are not exempt from using blind faith.

Stephen Hawking in, *The Grand Design* states on page 8, "The universes created *themselves* out of *nothing.*" [Emphasis added]. Christians are mocked for believing God always has been and always will be and that He created the universe out of nothing. Yet, the atheist walks relatively free, sometimes with their nose in the air, believing that there was literally nothing and then, *something.*[10]

Faith? Anyone? Bueller? Of course, there are many proposed guesses as to what happened prior to the Big Bang, but they are just that, guesses. Regarding the question of origin, both the Christian and atheist are in the same boat, and that boat has the same name, "faith."

A major difference, however, is that Christians recognize the place of faith in their worldview, while some atheists deny it. For many atheists, they will not be caught using such an infantile word such as faith!

Most people believe, Christians included, that the Big Bang is settled science. That it isn't, in fact, 'settled' can easily be demonstrated. If the Big Bang was settled science, why are there multiple explanations for the origin of the universe? Why are cosmologist and physicists calling the Big Bang into question if it is settled?

The Universe Forum, produced for NASA by the Harvard Smithsonian Center for Astrophysics contains an article that addresses the question, "What powered the Big Bang?"[11]

> Although astronomers understand what the universe was like just a few seconds after the Big Bang, no one yet knows what happened at the instant of the Big Bang—or what came before. What powered the Big Bang? Where did all the stuff in the universe come from in the first place? What was the universe like just before the Big Bang?
>
> But what *was* this primordial form of energy? And where did the "seed" of space and energy come from in the first place? How did the universe begin? The ultimate mystery is inspiring new ideas and new experiments. No one knows how the first space,

---

[10] My eleven-year old daughter and I were having a conversation on the origins of the universe. When I presented her with the idea that there was literally nothing, then something, she responded, "Wait, that doesn't make any sense." She proceeded to beckon her brother into the room saying, "Listen to this, it doesn't make any sense."

[11] https://www.cfa.harvard.edu/seuforum/bb_whatpowered.htm

time, and matter arose. And scientists are grappling with even deeper questions. If there was nothing to begin with, then where did the laws of nature come from? How did the universe "know" how to proceed? And why do the laws of nature produce a universe that is so hospitable to life? As difficult as these questions are, scientists are attempting to address them with bold new ideas—and new experiments to test those ideas.

Scientists are applauded for their continued efforts to explain the world we live in. Christians though, should not shy away from believing that God always has been and always will be.

Some hold the position that it is more rational and logical to believe God always has been and always will be and is responsible for the creation of the universe as opposed to there being nothing, then something, or, many universes creating themselves "out of nothing."

If it is true that finite things exist and cannot bring themselves into existence, and the universe had a beginning, it is fair to ask how the universe came into existence. Using the reasoning of the cosmological argument, it is also fair to posit the idea that because the universe had a beginning and could not have created itself out nothing, someone, who is uncaused, who is outside of time and space, is responsible for the finite universe we live in. We call Him, God.

Chapter 2

God's Existence: Design Argument

A few days into discussing toothpicks and the cosmological argument, brains begin to hurt. Toothpicks and the universe are finite, having a beginning and therefore, a creator who caused them into existence.

The cosmological argument for God's existence makes more sense than the alternative: there was nothing and then, boom,[12] there was something.

How else might we use the toothpicks to demonstrate God's existence? That is the next prompt provided to students. The last physical object they want to see on their desk are more toothpicks. Creativity is what we are looking for with this next argument. True to form, students pick up where they left off and begin designing words or objects on their desks with toothpicks. The answer is literally in front of their faces.

"Any ideas on how else to demonstrate God's existence with these toothpicks?" asks student one.

Student two, amid making a complex design on their desk responds, "No clue."

To assist the students in solving the problem, pages 101-102 from *I Don't Have Enough Faith to Be an Atheist* by Norman L. Geisler and Frank Turek are provided.[13] Geisler and Turek introduce the students to the Anthropic Principle, which is the concept that earth has been finely tuned for man's existence. The authors explain the principle on page 96:

> Scientists are now finding that the universe in which we live is like that diamond-studded Rolex, except the universe is even more precisely designed than the watch. In fact, the universe is specifically tweaked to enable life on earth—a planet with scores of improbable and interdependent life-supporting conditions that make it a tiny oasis in a vast and hostile universe. These highly precise and interdependent environmental conditions (which are called "anthropic constants") make up what is known as the

---

[12] Keeping the students on their toes, "boom" is spoken loud enough for the entire school to hear. After having been startled by the loud noise, many students jump a few inches in their seats. Those who suffered the most surprise spend the rest of the year wondering if I will do it again.

[13] Turek's https://crossexamined.org/ is a valuable resource for Christians looking for apologetical material put into practice and atheists looking for answers.

"Anthropic Principle." "Anthropic" comes from a Greek word that means "human" or "man." The Anthropic Principle is just a fancy title for the mounting evidence that has many scientists believing that the universe is extremely fine-tuned (designed) to support human life here on earth.

One example of an anthropic constant that supports human life is provided on page 102:

> Its [Gravity] strength may be terrifying, but it couldn't be any different for life to exist here on earth.
>
> If the gravitational force were altered by 0.0000000000000000000000000000000000001 percent, our sun would not exist, and, therefore, neither would we. Talk about precision.

Following the assigned reading, students are once again partnered up and instructed to use the toothpicks to demonstrate God's existence. Rational thought is now connected to the works of art created earlier on their desks. "Let's say I picked up these toothpicks and dropped them on the floor. What is the probability that they will land on the ground as a three-dimensional house?" confidently asks the student of their partner, who in turn laughs at the impossibility. Three-dimensional homes aside, what about the probability that the toothpicks land in a way that spells "faith?" Or make a perfect square?

Clothing lines are named after designers. No one believes that clothes randomly 1) appeared out of nowhere on their own 2) designed themselves into a fashionable item of glitzy colors and styles (even over millions of years). Cars have specific designs because they have designers. If the universe is designed, it must have a designer.

Geisler and Turek provide other examples of fine tuning including the interaction between the earth and the moon, atmospheric transparency, and earth's carbon dioxide and oxygen levels. Other examples include the ridiculous complexity of the eye and how it works in concert with the human brain, allowing you to see in front of you or to your side. Or, the complexity of the human brain and how it works in concert with the nervous system to let you know that you stubbed your toe, and the resulting pain is unappreciated. It is not just one piece of design that we are weighing as evidence for a designer, but literally hundreds, if not thousands of marks of design, all working together. Students are quick to note that not only does the universe seem to show marks of design, but the probability the universe created itself out of nothing *and* demonstrates design is too high to be the result of a random, cosmic explosion.

Not everyone agrees with that conclusion. Atheists do not go down without swinging, and I let the students know exactly how they swing back by introducing them to atheist, Richard Dawkins. In his bestselling book, *The God Delusion,* Dawkins illustrates the atheistic response to what seems to be a purposed and designed universe:

> Now, suppose the origin of life, the spontaneous arising of something equivalent to DNA, really was a quite staggeringly improbable event. Suppose it was so improbable as to occur on only one in a billion planets. A grant giving body would laugh at any chemist who admitted that the chance of his proposed research succeeding was only one in a hundred. But here we are talking about odds of one in a billion. And yet . . . even with such absurdly long odds, life will still have arisen on a billion planets—of which Earth, of course, is one.[14]

According to Dawkins and other atheists, we simply got lucky. Mere probability explains our existence! This conclusion is a far cry from anthropic principles discussed by Geisler and Turek. Gravitational force being spot on? Probability. Oxygen levels being just right? Probability. The elaborate interaction between the earth and the moon? Probability. Atmospheric transparency? Probability. The design of the human body and each of its individual parts working in harmony? Probability. This same human body working in concert with the elaborate set-up of the earth it exists within? Probability. Those conditions all working together over time, whether immediately created in one moment or evolved over time to make it look designed is only a matter of probability. How do we know this? We are here, are we not? And the consequences of the two positions carry significant implications for the Christian and atheist. Sentiments echoed in Dawkins's book, *River Out of Eden,* page 133:

> In a universe of electrons and selfish genes, blind physical forces and genetic replication, some people are going to get hurt, other people are going to get lucky, and you won't find any rhyme or reason in it, nor any justice. The universe that we observe has precisely the properties we should expect if there is, at bottom, no design, no purpose, no evil, no good, nothing but pitiless indifference.

---

[14] Richard Dawkins, *The God Delusion,* page 138

The universe is behaving exactly how it should if it is the result of mere chance; no design, no purpose, nothing but pitiless indifference! Where a Christian sees purpose, design, and creativity, the atheist sees millions of years of blind evolution which is a view that secular universities advocate in classrooms and is echoed on television, in movies, and everywhere else between. It is as they say, "settled science." You are an ignorant fool if you believe different than the establishment.

Do not tell that to former atheist James D. Agresti. His book, *Rational Conclusions* exposes the premise that the Big Bang and Darwinian evolution is settled science.

Agresti allows the reader to see a perspective ignored by many: doubt and uncertainty. Time permitting, Applied students read a few pages of his outstanding work in class, allowing them the opportunity to digest actual words of secular atheists who doubt what many assume to be true.

John C. Lennox's, *God's Undertaker: Has Science Buried God?* also takes to task the atheist who suggests science has settled the conversation on both the origins of the universe and the luck of the draw conclusion held by many non-believers. Agresti and Lennox provide ample evidence as to why a Christian should not swallow the evolution pill so quickly. But, both Agresti and Lennox are Christians. Students appreciate their Christian perspective, but they want a secular response that is not quoted in a Christian text.

After comparing the two approaches to the apparent design of the world (God versus probability and evolution over millions of years), students are shown, TheThirdWayofEvolution.com. I already stated that most assume biological evolution is settled science. Yet, not every secular atheist agrees:

> Even today, the public, and many scientists, are not aware of decades of research in evolutionary science, molecular biology and genome sequencing which provide alternative answers to how novel organisms have originated in the long history of life on earth. This web site is dedicated to making the results of that research available and to offering a forum to expose novel scientific thinking about the evolutionary process. The DNA record does not support the assertion that small random mutations are the main source of new and useful variations. We now know that the many different processes of variation involve well-regulated cell action on DNA molecules

Stephen Meyer's insightful tome, *Darwin's Doubt*, highlights the inadequacies of biological evolution and destroys the assumption that Darwinian evolution is settled science.

As one might imagine, students have never heard Darwinian evolution is questioned, and certainly not by a secular society of scientists which allegedly relies only on empirical science. Knowledge of this magnitude seems worthy of sharing with students, but The Third Way authors may disagree:

> It has come to our attention that THE THIRD WAY web site is wrongly being referenced by proponents of Intelligent Design and creationist ideas as support for their arguments. We intend to make it clear that the website and scientists listed on the web site do not support or subscribe to any proposals that resort to inscrutable divine forces or supernatural intervention, whether they are called Creationism, Intelligent Design, or anything else.

But why *not* reference atheists who question classical Darwinian evolution?

Comments from THE THIRD WAY are not shared to prove creationism, but to demonstrate that Darwinian evolution is not settled science as taught and assumed. Wasn't that what THE THIRD WAY people wanted conveyed?

Christian elementary schools have properly instructed students of God's responsibility for the universe. He designed the universe in such a way so that mankind, God's special creation could exist. Eventually, students begin to question. Instead of shielding students from opposing views, they are brought into the classroom. We read Sam Harris. We read Richard Dawkins.

One day, an atheist (and sadly other Christians) may accuse my students of being brainwashed and never exposed to differing ideas. Not the case in Applied! Opposing views are not hidden. The reader, and the student of Applied, is left on their own to contemplate which conclusion makes more sense: God's providence or mere probability.

The choice is theirs and only theirs. It is yours as well. Preceding our shift into the third argument for God's existence, a hidden image awaits their eyes with a prompt:

You are walking alone on the beach and you come across…

… when seeing this sandcastle[15] what questions come to mind?

The questions are predictable.

1) Who made it?
2) Who designed it?
3) Where did it come from?

In typical Horvath fashion, a question is offered in response, "What makes you think it was designed or made by someone?"

Point made.

No one believes the sandcastle independently and spontaneously popped into existence, out of nothing, or that its design was the product of millions of years of evolution. The Christian, when observing the universe, sees a massive and beautiful sandcastle which demands an answer to the obvious question: Who is the designer?

[15] Image by Stephane Abando from Pixabay.

Chapter 3

God's Existence: The Ontological Argument

The Ontological Argument for God's existence is not a favorite of mine. I find the cosmological and design arguments more compelling. Most students come to the same conclusion on their own volition.

It is rare you will hear me answer the question, "What do you think, Mr. Horvath?" Instead of answering their question for them, data and information is provided which will place the students in a position to make an informed and rational conclusion. Biblical questions are answered with Scripture, not Mr. Horvath's opinion.

In this spirit, then, students are left to their own to deliberate the Ontological argument's strength and effectiveness.

Ontology is the study of being or essence.

God, by definition, according to philosopher and theologian Anslem, is a being that no greater being can be conceived of by human thought. One may try, but you cannot think of a greater being than God. If you did think of a greater being than God, then that would be God. Modern apologists Alvin Plantinga and William Lane Craig argue that if it is possible that a Maximally Great entity exists, then mere possibility entails actual existence.

There is more to the argument, but one gets the point: God's essence and character are more than one can conceive of on their own; and His essence and character (ontology) cannot be exceeded by another. In Applied, the ontological argument is an opportunity to reintroduce God's nature and character. Anselm's argument is connected to the cosmological argument to counter a common atheistic line of reasoning.

Permit me to embark briefly on a tangent.

Standard assessments that require Scantron do not work well in Applied.[16] Plain matching and multiple-choice questions fail at measuring the magnitude of topics discussed in Applied. I was assigned the task of preparing graduating students for their transition from high school to college, from college to life. Scantron tests on the existence of God would not adequately prepare students for a real conversation about God's existence. Rather than using Scantron, or even a short answer essay, students are asked to create mock conversations between a Christian and atheist. Imagine you are sitting in a popular restaurant or cafe and your study partner notices the cross around your neck. Confused as to how a smart person could believe in God, they ask for your

---

[16] Scantron sheets require bubbling in circles for the correct answer of a T/F, multiple choice, or matching question.

reasoning.

Using the cosmological and design argument, create a back and forth conversation between yourself and your questioning friend. Guiding their conversation is a rubric containing necessary concepts and terms.

Christian: You have a cell phone?
Atheist: Of course.
Christian: Mind if I borrow it briefly?
Atheist: All yours my friend.
Christian: (The Christian pulls up an image of a sandcastle on their browser) Imagine you are walking on the beach and no one else is around. You see an intricate, three or four-story sandcastle. What questions would come to mind when seeing the sandcastle?
Atheist: Where did it come from? Who made it? Or, "Wow! Look at that design!"
Christian: Exactly, what's the probability that the sandcastle created itself into its current form?

The mock conversations are normally a page or two and are considered the written portion of their test. Written scripts will be turned in at my desk where a one-on-one verbal assessment awaits the students. Playing the role of the skeptical friend, I become their test. Their assignment is to put into practice learned content in conversational form against their instructor.

A handful of students become terrified at the prospect of having to talk to me. Most have never had a conversation with an atheist. Now, they are expected to go head to head with little 'old Mr. Horvath,' who according to student feedback is initially viewed as intimidating and intense.

Public speaking and coping with confrontation are not normally student strengths. Verbal assessments require students to both know and apply their knowledge in conversational form under pressure and unnerved. Verbal assessments are my favorite assessment tool. In college or the workplace, students will not be able to rely on multiple choice Scantron tests. Purses and briefcases will be void of any written script created in Applied. Interpersonal communication will be required for future face to face conversations with friends, roommates, colleagues, or companions. Preparation for these conversations is imperative. This level of preparation is why my annual contract is millions of dollars.[17]

Why this pedagogical tangent?

Presenting the ontological argument as, "Nothing greater than God

[17] And if you believe that...

can be conceived," leads students and skeptics to interpret the argument to mean, "Whatever I think of can be god? Why can't I just believe in the Flying Spaghetti Monster (FSM)?" After finishing their first written script between atheist and Christian, students are required to end their conversation with a common question or snarky challenge, "Well, why can't I just believe in the FSM?" Their question acts as a transition from the cosmological and design arguments into the ontological argument. So, why not the FSM?

A couple reasons. When deliberating the cosmological argument, we were sure to use the word "finite," meaning limited by time and space. God is outside of time and space. He is not finite. If God were limited by time and space, He would not be God. Our friendly FSM is finite. Images of the FSM consist of spaghetti and meatballs, all of which are finite. Furthermore, these finite objects were created by finite creators, humans.

This is not to say people believe the FSM to be real. They do not. Instead, the FSM has become a way to mock a Christian's conclusion affirming God's existence. "You can believe in God, we will believe in the FSM," is the sentiment. Fine, but my Garbage Disposal Deity will destroy your FSM in less than ten seconds. And the Christian God who is not limited by time and space, who always has been and always will be, will destroy any finite creation, Pink Unicorns included, that the atheist posits as a competitor.

Second, exhibiting marks of design indicates the FSM has a designer. Design requires a designer and a creator. If someone, or something designed and brought the FSM into existence, the FSM cannot be God.

If no greater being than God can be conceived, then what specifically is great about this God? Traditional Christian theology argues (simplified), God is all-knowing, all-present, all-powerful, loving, just, kind, pure, holy, blameless, morally superior, and so forth. You cannot be more loving than an all-loving God. If you can think of an entity more loving, then that would be God. God is the ceiling of greatness that we think of and confess. The FSM can never match the ontology of the creator of the universe which resides outside of time and space.

Discussing the ontological argument for God's existence naturally flows from the first two arguments, which is why it is addressed. Perhaps God is the Uncaused Cause of all causes and is also responsible for the design of the universe. But if God does exist, is He a good God? What's His nature? And how does His nature influence the Christian worldview and how its manifested in the world we live in?

I want to be clear: Applied uses the ontological argument as an opportunity to discuss the nature and character of God *as opposed to using the argument to prove God's existence*. God's nature and character is a necessary conversation that secures a foundation for future discussions such as morality, dating and relationships. For this reason, it is imperative that we address His putative nature, not merely His existence. For example, His nature is called into question by Christians and atheist alike when they ask the common question, "Why would a loving God let bad things happen to good people?"

Nonetheless, the ontological argument helps address God's character while knocking down sophomoric attempts to compare God to the FSM.

With that said, it is worth pointing out that some people may yet find value in the argument as it pertains to ascertaining God's existence.

As alluded to above, the intrinsic problem to the Flying Spaghetti Monster retort to Christian theism is that you can easily imagine something greater than it. However, if the reader would recall, in chapter one I brought up the problem of the 'infinite regress.'[18] That problem raises its head here, too.

With an 'infinite regress' not possible in reality, then even as we invoke the 'highest thing we can imagine' we must acknowledge and conclude there is something which is uniquely different than everything that came before it, as C.S. Lewis puts it, *sui generis*.[19]

Thus, we reasoned that only things with a beginning had a cause but realized at some point we needed to invoke something unique in its nature, an uncaused cause, or a 'prime' mover.

Here again we land on territory where even non-Christians have trod. The famed and ancient philosopher, Aristotle, engaged in this exact same reasoning and concluded, quite independently of Christianity, that reasonable people must conclude there exist an 'uncaused cause,' and deduced certain attributes to this entity which, as it happens, comport in many respects with what Christianity says, as well.

But Christianity does not have Reason only. It also has Revelation it can draw on. But that is a different chapter! Nonetheless, while I want to be quite clear that my point of raising the ontological argument is to introduce the question of God's nature, some people may find fertile ground for reconciling some of their doubts by studying the ontological argument in more depth.

Readers interested in learning more about the philosophical leanings of the ontological argument can visit William Lane Craig's webpage, reasonablefaith.org.[20]

---

[18] In Chapter 1, Premise 4 and following.
[19] C. S. Lewis, *The Abolition of Man*, Chapter 3.
[20] https://www.reasonablefaith.org/ontological/

Chapter 4

God's Existence:
The Moral Law Argument and the Question of Pain

Discussing the origins and design of the universe offers a natural segue into addressing God's nature and character, which in turn, offers a natural transition into introducing a fourth argument for God's existence, the 'moral law' argument.

We will introduce and apply the moral law in three parts:

1. The moral argument itself
2. The secular moral conundrum(s)
3. Why would a loving God allow bad things to happen to good people?

Part 1: The Moral Law Argument assumes a source

Non-believers and believers often challenge the character of God by asking a common question:

> "If God does exist (cosmological and design argument) and is so great (ontological argument), then why would he let bad things happen to good people?"

Applied Christianity and Applied recognize we are finite humans limited to time, space, and knowledge. Our perspective is myopic compared to one who not only resides outside of time and space, but also created space. Trying to answer this question with our limited perspective is difficult. Some suggest not spending time on the question at all. But a fair question deserves a fair response. Ignoring the question and leaving graduating seniors to confront the dilemma for the first time in their philosophy class, is a great disservice.

If a Christian is asking the question, using Scripture will be of obvious benefit. However, a non-believer would find using Scripture less than impressive. In class, Sam Harris's (atheist) book, *Letter to a Christian Nation* is utilized as an introduction to the question.

In his book, Harris challenges God's greatness and moral superiority. If God were loving, argues Harris, then why was the Holocaust permitted? Where was God on 9/11? If God is loving, why would He not prevent rape?

Having read a couple pages of Harris's work, students are partnered up and provided a few moments to find a solution to the dilemma.

Struggling independently from instructor influence is critical. They are the ones who will be heading off to college soon and interacting with arguments against their worldview, not me. After a few moments, the class is brought back together for a larger conversation where the experienced instructor can offer wisdom, knowledge, and insight.[21]

The most common answer provided is 'sin.' This is theologically correct. Christianity posits that we live in a fallen world. Living in a fallen world leaves tragic consequences. Scriptural answers do not carry weight with an atheist who rejects God and the concept of sin. Therefore, students are asked to consider other possible responses which may encourage the atheist to reconsider their question.

This is a difficult task considering students have not taken any philosophy classes yet. Most seniors will take a philosophy class for the first time in college where God's existence and morality are almost certain to be introduced and challenged. Applied recognizes this reality and introduces students to possible philosophical responses to the question.

One response requires an introduction to one of the premier Christian apologists in the world, Ravi Zacharias.[22] Ravi speaks across the world and is involved in a plethora of question and answer forums every year, most of which are recorded and posted on the Internet for viewing. On this day, students are shown a video of Ravi responding to the question of evil and why God would allow it. Ravi puts forward this line of reasoning:

Premise 1: If you are saying there is evil, you are saying there is good (to compare evil against)
Premise 2: If you are saying there is evil and good, you are saying there is a moral law from which you are making this moral conclusion
Premise 3: If there is a moral basis, you are positing a moral law giver.
Conclusion: That moral law giver is God.

Restated: If there is no moral law giver, there is no moral law, if there is no moral law, there is no good or evil, if there is no good and evil, how can you accuse God of being immoral? As Ravi rightly claims the argument self-destructs without a moral basis.

Students are encouraged to answer moral accusations against God, Christians, or the Scriptures by asking the accuser, "On what basis?"

---

[21] This is, of course, why I get paid millions of dollars.
[22] https://www.rzim.org/

Atheist: If God was good, He would not let bad things happen.
Christian: On what basis?
Atheist: What?
Christian: You are an atheist?
Atheist: Yes
Christian: What moral basis are you using to accuse God of immoral behavior?

First, notice the challenger assumes God's nature and character (ontological argument) to be all-knowing, all-powerful, loving, just, etc. Second, the challenger assumes God's existence. Third, they are using a moral code in their accusation, which is problematic for a non-believer. Step one introduces students to the moral law syllogism and the need for a source. Step two challenges the non-believer's source for morality if it is not God.

Part 2: The Secular Moral Conundrum(s)
The Moral Law Argument assumes human value

Two questions are asked of the students:

1. Is murder wrong?
2. Is rape wrong?

Stunned students answer in the affirmative, but their initial answers to the follow up question lack substance, "Why is rape or murder wrong?" Classic responses range from "Because it is." or, "Because consent matters." The only reason rape is wrong is because it goes against consent? That is the *only* reason? Seriously? "Well, it's against the law." Our government says it is wrong, therefore it is wrong? Yikes. Another common response is, "The Bible says so." Prompting my response, "*Why* does God in His Scripture oppose rape and murder?

In the summer of 2019, I received an email from a friend of a graduate asking why I believed in God. As part of the conversation, the emailer was asked the questions above regarding rape and murder, resulting in this response, "Any action that hurts another human being, in order to gratify yourself, is morally wrong." But, *why?*[23] Applying the moral law syllogism, on what moral basis is it morally wrong to gratify yourself at the expense of others? Second, from an atheistic

---

[23] When pushed further on why rape is morally wrong, the questioner responded, "because that's what society says." At this point of the conversation, the reasons given as to why rape is morally wrong is because 1) it hurts people and 2) society says so. The questions remain: 1) W*hy* does violating another human matter? 2) *What* is the moral basis being used to make this conclusion?

point of view, why does protecting innocent human life matter?

Juxtapose murder and rape with Richard Dawkins's quote from *River Out of Eden*, page 133:

> In a universe of electrons and selfish genes, blind physical forces and genetic replication, some people are going to get hurt, other people are going to get lucky, and you won't find any rhyme or reason in it, nor any justice. The universe that we observe has precisely the properties we should expect if there is, at bottom, no design, no purpose, no evil, no good, nothing but pitiless indifference.

In other words, there is no objective moral law or standard provided by an improbable and random cosmic explosion. Read Dawkins's quote again and look for a source of intrinsic rights and morality within the atheistic worldview. As argued by Sam Harris and others, no metaphysical or spiritual moral law exists. Morality is whatever is "best" for society or the individual.

Harris's position has limitations. What does "best" mean? And does not "best" assume there is a "worst?" Where did that basis come from? Lacking a moral law and a moral law giver, morality is left in the hands of the individual, majority rule and government. Morality becomes subjective to each person and government. What I find to be morally acceptable another person, or government, may not.

On the surface this seems noble, but deeper introspection highlights obvious concerns. I may find it morally acceptable to steal your possessions, whereas you do not. Perhaps my family, which is rather large, finds it acceptable to control one large area of land that someone else owns. One government may view the Holocaust acceptable (Germany) and others may not (America). Which government is correct? Ask any non-believer and it will be the government that protects human life. But, why should human life be protected? On what basis is it bad to murder human life and good to protect innocent human life? Secular individuals are forced to recognize that not only is morality one-hundred percent subjective but so too is the value of human life.

Bad things happening to good people, or God allowing bad things to happen to good people, not only assumes a moral basis, but it also assumes people ought to be protected from that which is bad. Why? According to the world, humans possess value and human rights that should be protected. But, in the atheistic worldview, what is the source for intrinsic value and rights of humans? If no spiritual or metaphysical source exists, the value of human life becomes subjective to either government dictates or individual choice.

A student once asked, "Why can't I give myself rights and value?" Child of God,[24] you can and that is my point. You can give yourself as many rights and as much value as you want, but that does not mean everyone is obligated to agree with your decision. Murderers and rapist assign their victims less value than they give themselves. Yes, you can give yourself value, but not everyone has to agree with your declarative value. A nonbeliever's value (and rights) comes not from an intrinsic source, but rather subjective and external standards such as the government, outward beauty, parent's approval, academic, athletic, or monetary success.[25] No other source exists other than external standards, and that is dangerous.

Not only does the moral law argument challenge the atheist's source and subjectivity of morality, but it points to an obvious conclusion: humans have a special type of value

> that every other creation in the world fails to possess
> that ought to be morally protected at the highest level

Ravi Zacharias draws an important distinction between animals and humans: the question of evil (and essentially intrinsic value) is always asked *by* a person or *about* a person.[26]

No one screams bloody murder when a squirrel lies dead on the road.[27] Roadkill is scooped up and tossed into the trash or used for research. Dispatch remains silent when a tourist observes a lion devouring a hyena. Yet, with humans, if someone shoots someone else for standing on the wrong sidewalk tile, 911 would be called. Why? Innocent human life is morally different than that of a squirrel, hyena,

---

[24] A Mr. Horvath catch phrase meant to convey exasperation or incredulity.

[25] No one should be confused as to why our youth struggle with anxiety and depression so much. We have convinced them they are nothing more than evolved animals living meaningless lives, waiting to die, and become worm food.

[26] There are those who try to put animals and humans on the same level. Christians recognize that mankind was made in the image of God and have a special place above animals. Atheists who try to ascribe intrinsic or extrinsic value to animals contradict their own worldview that, "there is, at bottom, no design, no purpose, no evil, no good, nothing but pitiless indifference." Evolutionary hierarchy mandates that the higher evolved, stronger, and more fit animal uses the less evolved or sophisticated animal at their disposal.

[27] This point is made obvious in the classroom as I throw either a shoe or a Kleenex box at the classroom door. Students look at me in bewilderment, wondering what is wrong their teacher. No one calls 911 or runs to the office out of respect for the shoe or box. However, when I pretend to assault a student, their reactions change from bewilderment to momentary fear and concern for their classmate. Why? Because human life is different than any other life, or non-life.

or lion. If someone disagrees, they should be challenged as to why they are not trying to save hyenas from lions, flies from spiders, or mice from cats.

The Romans, Greeks, and Jews all knew innocent human life ought to be protected, even if their method of addressing the murderer differed. Aztecs, when sacrificing to their gods, predominately used captured enemies. They were not walking down Main Street pulling random Aztecs out of their homes and murdering them at will. They knew murder of their own people was unacceptable.

What woman in any culture believed rape to be an acceptable norm that they should go along with? They knew they were being violated, even if the suspect felt otherwise. We are justifiably outraged if a woman (or male) is raped. If we are on safari and witness a male lion mount a lioness to engage in sexual reproduction, we chuckle until our kids ask, "What is he doing to the other lion, Dad?" Does anyone call 911 and accuse the lion of rape? Of course not. Where is PETA or the ACLU? Is PETA launching campaigns to protect lions from devouring their prey or mounting a lioness? Is the ACLU fighting for the safety of hyenas? Why not? The answer is obvious: human value supersedes that of any animal's value.

God deems murder and rape to be morally unacceptable in the Bible not because He arbitrarily demands such, but because murder and rape violate the image of God each person bears. "God created mankind in His own image, in the image of God he created them; male and female He created them."[28] Despite the erroneous claims made by skeptics of Christianity, Christianity elevates mankind's status in a way the atheistic worldview does not and cannot. We are more than our DNA and should be treated accordingly.

Christianity's moral law argument for God's existence demonstrates that not only is there a moral law, but humans possess intrinsic value that ought to be protected. And, if humans possess intrinsic value (or rights) that ought to be protected, they must also have an intrinsic value giver, God. Apart from God, humanity is reduced to nothing more than matter. How does an improbable, cosmic explosion create special intrinsic value (or rights) in humans that should be protected? The question of morality assumes what atheism cannot provide, intrinsic human value and a moral basis from which it should be protected.

Let us apply our insight to the email received over the summer:

---

[28] Genesis 1:27

"Any action that hurts another human being, in order to gratify yourself, is morally wrong."

Taking atheism to its logical conclusion, as supplied by Richard Dawkins, on what basis is it morally wrong to hurt another human if morality, good and evil, do not exist? What is it about a human that makes it worth protecting? Atheism struggles to provide adequate, convincing, and consistent answers outside of external standards.

In class we argue that a theistic approach makes a better case for protecting human life than atheism. We can make that case without referencing Christian Scripture:

> If God does exist and He is the Uncaused Cause of all causes and is responsible for creating the world and designing it especially for humans, then the Uncaused Cause, that is, God, is responsible for creating human life. If God is responsible for creating human life, then human life belongs to God. If human life belongs to God, (all knowing, all-powerful, loving, just, etc.) innocent human life which is a manifestation of that creator has intrinsic value and ought to be protected.

Compared to the atheistic worldview, most students side with a theistic approach because they do not believe they, and the rest of the universe, are the result of an improbable cosmic explosion. Exactly why students should believe it to be the *Christian* God is discussed throughout the school year (as well as in their junior theology class).

Now that we have returned to the emailer's question, and with Dawkins's quote in mind, let us revisit the initial question posted by Sam Harris and other non-believers, "Why would a loving God let bad things happen to good people?"

1. The question assumes human life has value that should be protected from bad things happening.
2. What moral basis is he using to determine if something is good or bad?
3. How can God be immoral if there is no moral basis from which to make that accusation?
4. What makes you think good or bad people exist if there is no good or evil?

Atheists that accuse God of being immoral must provide a moral basis from which they are making their accusation, an accusation which assumes the existence of good and evil. But the existence of good and evil is one of the things that they deny. Remember, according to

Richard Dawkins, the existence of good and evil is excluded on their own worldview:

> The universe that we observe has precisely the properties we should expect if there is, at bottom, no design, no purpose, no evil, no good, nothing but pitiless indifference.

If there is no God, "no design, no purpose, no evil, no good, nothing but pitiless indifference," there is then, in atheism, no objective moral law from which the accusation carries weight. Eighteen-year old youth are astute enough to see how the logical contradiction in the atheistic view does not exist in the opposite view: If God does exist, there *is* design, purpose, evil, good and a moral law written upon our hearts.

Discussing objective morality and intrinsic value does not empirically make God appear in the classroom, "proving His existence." However, God's existence offers what atheism and naturalism cannot provide, objective morality connected to objective intrinsic moral value and worth.

Part 3: But what about the bad things happening to good people?

Granting the existence of God and a moral law, their question remains, "Mr. Horvath, can you elaborate on why God, if He is in fact loving (ontological argument), would let bad things happen to good people?"

In class, the question is addressed from both a Biblical and philosophical point of view because they will soon be graduating and interacting with both Christians and non-Christians alike. Addressing the question appropriately depends on the worldview of the questioner, a fact that students themselves need to consider as they get older.

Above, we began to answer the question as if a non-believer were asking. Basically, we challenged the non-believer's right to ask the question at all, because they were assuming for their question the very thing they denied existed. That is called "having one's cake and eating it too." Now, we will focus on potential Christian responses.

One response allows me to introduce students to former atheist C.S. Lewis and his popular work, *The Screwtape Letters*. It is the first time Lewis is introduced to the class by name. *The Screwtape Letters* contain thirty-one fictional letters authored by Screwtape who is instructing his nephew, Wormword, on how to move his patient away from a belief in God. Each letter contains a carefully constructed plan of attack for Wormwood to implement. Lewis, via Screwtape, reminds us that humans have both mountain top experiences and low points in life, referred to as troughs. Why would God let His child experience troughs? Screwtape educates Wormwood,

> Merely to over-ride a human will (as His felt presence in any but the faintest and most mitigated degree would certainly do) would be for Him [God] useless. *He cannot ravish. He can only woo.* He wants them to learn to walk and must therefore take away His hand; and if only the will to walk is there He is pleased even with their stumbles. Do not be deceived, Wormwood. Our cause is never more in danger than when a human, no longer desiring, but still intending, to do our Enemy's will, looks round upon a universe from which every trace of Him seems to have vanished, and asks why he has been forsaken, and still obeys. [Emphasis added]

Prior to digging deeper, students are provided ten questions, three of which are below and best represent the larger point of the ten:

1. Would you consider causing or allowing your child to experience pain and suffering?
2. Would you allow someone else to cause your child pain and suffering?
3. Are you against keeping your child locked in their bedrooms for their entire life?

If you answered, yes, yes, and no, you passed the test. Parents may cause their child pain when smacking their hand away from a hot stove, but they do it anyway because parents know something the child does not: a burned hand is far worse than one that stings briefly from a swat. Often, children learning how to walk or ride a bike fall and get hurt. However, if the parent held on to the bike forever, the child may never learn to ride it at all.

Vaccinations are provided to children on a regular basis, which hurt physically as well as mentally and emotionally. Children who participate in sports can expect a coach to exact high expectations in games, practices, and conditioning. Student athletes may become exhausted or suffer through warm summer days replete with opportunities for conditioning excellence.

Matter of fact, no one calls a parent immoral for encouraging their child to learn how to walk after experiencing pain after the first, second and third attempts. Parents sit in comfortable chairs while watching coaches run their children up and down the football field. Are they immoral for allowing their child to experience physical pain and mental suffering?

Neither is God immoral for allowing pain and suffering.

What *would* be immoral would be locking children up and never providing for them the opportunity to experience freedom and love, which, as anyone experienced with the world knows, often results in pain and suffering and yet *is worth it*.

Freedom comes at a price.

Elaborating on the point, in class I use a male student as analogy: Imagine you have a child whom from birth you have locked in a room with only a small window for natural light. He is fed three times a day. When able to communicate, he is only fed when speaking, "I love you" to his parents.

Parent: Good morning, John.
Child: Good morning, Dad.
Parent: Are you hungry?
Child: Yes Dad.
Parent: …waiting patiently…
Child: I love you.

The parent hands over the meal. This exact process occurs at breakfast, lunch, and dinner.

Parent: Ready for lunch, John?
Child: Yes Dad.
Parent: …waiting patiently….
Child: I love you.

By the time we get to dinner, the student assistant dramatically states his unequivocal love for his dad (me) before being asked if he is hungry. The analogy is followed with a question: Is the child expressing pure love?

No student concludes the child is expressing or experiencing genuine love towards or from his father. Why not? As the students will tell you, the child is being forced to say, "I love you."

Coerced love is not love. How do we solve this dilemma? The predictable student response is to let the child out of the room and experience freedom. But, says the teacher, if we let him out of the room, he may get hurt. Summoning their best Hallmark card voice, the students plead, "But at least he will be free to live and love freely." Exactly.

Forcing yourself on another person without their consent is rape. Forcing someone to spiritually love you against their will would be spiritual rape. Who wants God forcing love on His creation? Is that genuine love? Of course not. It would be unloving for God to force Himself on others; it would also be a contradiction to His nature.[29]

For His creation to truly love Him, God cannot ravish, He can only woo. He will give you freedom; freedom that carries consequences. One may reject God, like the child may reject their parents, a risk every parent takes when having a child. She may love her parents, or she may reject her parents. Aside from the risk of rejection, the child will also experience mental, emotional, physical, or spiritual pain. Regardless, the benefit is greater than the risk: real love.

Dawkins and his friends' alternatives are not encouraging. In atheism, "there is, at bottom, no design, no purpose, no evil, no good, nothing but pitiless indifference." On the same page Dawkins writes the words quoted above, he writes that humans dance to their DNA. Any action that takes place, any choice that you make that has a positive or negative reaction is the result of your DNA. Choice is removed as an option because your DNA is dictating your decisions, and therefore, your consequences. How is that for freedom? Try making a moral claim against anyone who claims they are dancing to their pre-determined DNA. "Your honor, I murdered this individual, but I was only dancing to my DNA. You surely cannot hold me accountable for who I am."

The second part of our answer to the question of why a loving God would let bad things happen to good people is:

1. If God truly is love, He must give His children freedom to love without coercion-otherwise, it is not love.
2. Within this freedom, His children unfortunately harm themselves and others. However, love is worth the risk.

When discussing the origins of the universe, most students conclude that it is more rational to believe God always has been, always will be, and is responsible for the creation of the universe, as opposed to there being nothing and then there being an improbable cosmic explosion. Likewise, students find God giving His creation freedom, a better option than determinism and spiritual coercion. Seeing it as an opportunity to introduce the love of God without necessarily using Scripture verses, students feel confident using this line of reasoning

[29] Another opportunity to relate the ontological argument and God's nature to the conversation.

with a secular-minded individual.

Theologically, the question takes a different approach. Students are partnered up and asked to identify multiple assumptions in the question, "Why would a loving God let bad things happen to good people?"

1. It assumes God's existence (see above)
2. It assumes bad things happen (see above)
3. It assumes good people exist
4. It assumes love exists

If the question assumes God's existence, it is only right that God gets a say in the answer. Part three of our response to the question uses Scripture and God's voice. Assuming God's existence, we use Scripture to address the assumption that good people exist, which, as it happens, is an assumption Christianity rejects.

Romans 3:11 states, "There is no one righteous, not even one; there is no one who understands; there is no one who seeks God." Tithing, educational status, or helping the needy does not establish one's goodness. No one person is greater than another. Christianity is clear, we are fallen sinners separated from God. I have seen strong, God-fearing men and women die to horrible diseases because of our sinful nature. Good people, from a Scriptural point of view, do not exist and no one can escape the consequences of sin, which is death (Romans 6:23).

The Good Lord created mankind in His image. Mankind was given freedom to choose God or choose themselves. This freedom carried consequences that are felt by the individual and all of creation.

Pastors and laymen included, try to find hope in tragedy by declaring "everything happens for a reason." As if God went out of His way to give millions of people cancer or ALS! Try telling a parent who lost their child, "everything happens for a reason." God, killed their child so that their faith could be strengthened? Everything does happen for a reason, sin.

God has a solution that deals squarely with the underlying problem, which is sin.

"Why would a loving God let bad things happen to good people?"

Only once in history did it happen where a truly good person had tragedy strike Him down for the sake of goodness. God's solution to our sin and its consequences is Christ. Tragedy, as manifested at the cross of Christ, saved, and redeemed a fallen and broken world.

One atheist student ironically suggested that our hearts recognize that there is a guiding voice within each of us that communicates a desire to believe in God. Quite right. It is this that explains why goodness, justice, hope, and love exist; that murder, rape, racism, and slavery are morally abhorrent. Not because God says so, *per se*, but because they violate the ingrained image of God which each human possesses

It is fair to remember that God's perspective is greater than ours. Applied uses human reason and philosophical arguments to address one of the toughest questions that has plagued man for centuries. There is no doubt that people have excruciatingly painful experiences which seem difficult to reconcile with the existence of a loving God, especially while they are enduring those experiences. History records much horror. Nonetheless, if we consider the matter dispassionately (preferably, before we are thrown into painful life experiences), we can comprehend the outline of the reality of things.

Scripture reminds us that no one is good; that all have fallen short of the glory of God; and that God, in His kindness and goodness has rescued us from our sin. I humbly recognize earthly limitations in answering the question and point us all to the cross of Christ which answers the question and problem of pain effectively and eternally.

> Surely, He took up our pain and bore our suffering, yet we considered him punished by God, stricken by Him, and afflicted. But He was pierced for our transgressions, He was crushed for our iniquities; the punishment that brought us peace was on Him, and by His wounds we are healed. We all, like sheep, have gone astray, each of us has turned to our own way; and the Lord has laid on Him the iniquity of us all.

Isaiah 53

Part II

Worldview Identification and Implications

Chapter 5

Worldview Identification

Besides God's revealed Word, world, and creation, there are strong reasons to recognize His existence. It makes sense that if the world had a beginning, a catalyst was needed. A catalyst that was not itself caused, but rather was and is, uncaused (cosmological argument). Earth's delicate dance with the sun and moon in perfect harmony, while simultaneously submitting to the physical laws of nature, cannot be dismissed as mere accident (design argument).

A designed universe requires a divine designer, which we refer to as God. If God does exist, His nature and character would have Him be that which always has been and always will be. He is the Holy of Holies, Light of Light, the Beginning, and the End (ontological argument). If the King of Kings created humans in His own image, we are image bearers of the Uncaused Cause of the universe. We are image bearers that ought to be highly valued and protected (moral law argument).

Christian Scriptures best align with the attributes one would expect God to possess. Students do not have to accept the arguments as presented. Conclusions on God's existence are their own, and are not coerced, although we strive to ensure their reasoning is valid. Regardless of their position, the next logical step in Applied's progression is to discuss their chosen worldview.

If you believe in God, your worldview influences every aspect of the life entrusted to you by God. Likewise, if you do not believe in God, your worldview influences the rest of your life according to that worldview. Your conclusion carries serious consequences and implications, like whether human life has intrinsic value and rights.

We are only talking about the rest of their lives; and their children's lives and *their* children's lives. After discussing God's existence, we explain how their worldview influences life. Per the usual, students are partnered up and asked to identify life's most important questions. Two prompts launch the investigation:

1. What is a worldview?
2. What questions does your worldview answer?

Lacking a definition of the term worldview causes consternation.[30]

---

[30] Knowledge and understanding of Bloom's taxonomy is just as important as evaluating and applying.

Placing the prompt in a context provides direction, "Imagine you and your friends are sitting around a campfire discussing life, what questions would you be trying to answer?" After coming up with their own guesses as to life's most important questions, we read two pages out of James Sire's, *The Universe Next Door*. Ravi Zacharias identifies four essential questions to life, on page 17 Sire introduces seven (echoed by Ravi):

1. What is prime reality?
2. What is the nature of external reality?
3. What is a human being?
4. What happens to a person after death?
5. Why is it possible to know anything at all?
6. How do we know what is right and wrong?
7. What is the meaning of human history?

These are hard hitting, deep, life influencing questions, that find their way onto our weekly memory quizzes. As we will see, they set the tone for many important topics discussed during the year. A theist and atheist answer these questions differently (as mentioned in our discussion of the moral law argument for God's existence).

In class we make a chart to show the difference between the two worldviews:

Question	Christian Worldview	Atheist Worldview
1. What is prime reality?	God	The Cosmos
2. What is the nature of external reality?	Orderly; spiritual, created by God	Chaos; material; dependent on the person
3. What is a human being?	A unique Child of God full of potential washed in the blood of Christ; Made in the image of God	An evolved animal; a naked ape
4. What happens to a person after death?	Either heaven or hell	Nothing; rots.
5. Why is it possible to know anything at all?	God has revealed Himself through general (nature) and special (His Word, miracles) revelation	Mankind's knowledge evolved as man evolved
6. How do we know what is right and wrong?	God's revealed Word as provided to us in written format as well as revealed upon our hearts (conscience)	Subjective and moral relativism rule the day; government decides who has rights and how those rights will be manifested
7. What is the meaning of human history?	Love God, love people, share the Gospel (Matthew 22); Advance the kingdom of God	Advance one's self and civilization

Our entire school year is applying these questions and their answers to our lives. Diving into specifics comes as units progress, but a few examples are initially offered.

One example that relates to many students is the death of a loved one. If you are an atheist, it contradicts your worldview to believe your deceased loved one is watching over you from above. This is a struggle for those who are angry with God and deny His existence, but still want to believe their loved one exists in a spiritual realm.

Let's apply the questions below:

The atheist rejects God (1) and therefore rejects a spiritual realm

(2). The material realm is the only realm to exist within. When the evolved individual (3) dies, he or she is left to decay (4). Hopefully, the individual lived a "good" (6) life worthy of reflection by his loved ones (7). Let's place the death of a loved one in the context of Richard Dawkins's now infamous quote:

> In a universe of electrons and selfish genes, blind physical forces and genetic replication, some people are going to get hurt, other people are going to get lucky, and you won't find any rhyme or reason in it, nor any justice. The universe that we observe has precisely the properties we should expect if there is, at bottom, no design, no purpose, no evil, no good, nothing but pitiless indifference.

Remember, *on their view*, death is the end of the road for the evolved human. One is left to wonder what a "good" life looks like from an atheistic point of view. Perhaps the individual found a cure for cancer, but then again, "some people are going to get hurt, others are going to get lucky, and you won't find any rhyme or reason in it…just pitiless indifference."[31]

Using the same example, we will contrast the atheistic worldview with the Christian worldview. The Christian recognizes God's existence (1) and therefore recognizes there is a spiritual realm (2) unseen to our eyes. Seeing that a human being has been made in the image of God and is a spiritual creation (3), and God is concerned for the spiritual well-being of His creation, when the human dies, life continues beyond the material realm and into the spiritual (4). Hopefully, the individual lived in a way that reflected the love of God so that others too may know His love (7).

As one might expect the difference between the two worldviews is enormous. "What's wrong with advancing society?" asked a student. Christians obviously don't object to the advancement of society so long as the advancement does not go against the will and dictates of God. Please, find the cure for cancer, heal the broken body, cure anxiety and depression so that mankind may live mentally and emotionally healthy lives as envisioned by their Creator. Whatever you do, do it for the glory of God (1 Corinthians 10:31). Advancing both the Kingdom of God and kingdom of man coexist within the Christian worldview. The purpose and reasoning behind the advancement is the sticking point between the Christian and atheistic worldview. As further

---

[31] Richard Dawkins, *River Out of Eden*, page 133

demonstrated below, the Christian argues that there is more to life than simply living out your DNA and arbitrarily helping society.

If only the animal kingdom exists, and we likewise are just animals, the world would lack love, romance, art, hope, justice, and fairness, etc., as things that exist *in reality*.

The naturalistic animal kingdom does not know love, hope, joy, service, art, romance, sadness, anger, betrayal, concepts of a Creator, etc. It knows survival, reproduction, death, and destruction.

When hyenas destroy their prey, no tribunal of accountability is held. When the sun rises in the face of the lion, he does not paint a beautiful picture in hopes of presenting his work to his lioness. The lioness upon receiving the work of art does not record a sonnet to be passed on from generation to generation. Birds of the air do not sing songs of joy and wonder in response to witnessing amazing, heart-throbbing romance. They make noises which disappear into the wind.

Human experience is uniquely that, human. Merely recognizing this insight is evidence that we are more than meets the eye.[32]

Depending on how one answers question three above, we are either walking DNA or specially created in the image of God (Genesis 1:26-27). The implications are staggering.

After identifying whether they are an atheist or theist and briefly looking at life's most important questions, students are directed to worldviewweekend.com where a lengthy survey awaits.

Individual results tend to split between moderate Biblical Christianity and secular humanism, bothering some students who profess they are rooted in Scripture. How could their results possibly be secular? Despite years of Christian education, most of these young men and women are naïve to the Scriptural positions on moral and ethical issues of the day.

Their worldview has been shaped by a predominantly secular society. Popular music and movies hardly relate to Christianity. Secularism has been normalized not just in society but unconsciously within each student. Alternatively, it is possible students know what Scripture declares as acceptable, but they prefer secular humanism instead.

Unfortunately, Christians spend most of their time reading the world into the Word rather than reading the Word into the world, with many Christians prioritizing earthly citizenship above their heavenly citizenship.

32 Another attempt at humor that earns a few eyerolls from those familiar with The Transformers

We do not have to look far for the reason. Young men and women (and adults) are not meditating on the Word of God during their summers or even in the school year. Various secular avenues are their primary source for entertainment, news, and truth.

Parents, who are primary influences of their children, tend to have a more secular approach to the world as well. Christian congregations have embraced a more secular approach to Christianity. It is my responsibility to teach what it looks like to have a worldview that starts at the cross and God's Word as opposed to the world. Much of the year is spent addressing false assumptions and beliefs about Christianity, ironically, many of them created by Christians. James Sire accurately represents my role when he writes,

> A worldview is composed of a number of basic presuppositions, more or less consistent with each other, more or less consciously held, more or less true. They are generally unquestioned by each of us, rarely, if ever mentioned by our friends, *and only brought to mind when we are challenged by a foreigner from another ideological universe.* [Emphasis added]

I am that foreigner from another ideological universe.

Many students start where secular society has directed them to begin. Applied, however, starts at the cross, with the living Word of God, in every topic of conversation.[33]

Two months into the year, we have completed building (or rebuilding) a foundation for the year and the rest of their lives. Does God exist? What is your worldview? How does your worldview answer life's most important questions? Once we have established a foundation, we begin to move forward into what it looks like to live one's worldview within specific content areas.

We begin by identifying key Biblical concepts using this diagram:

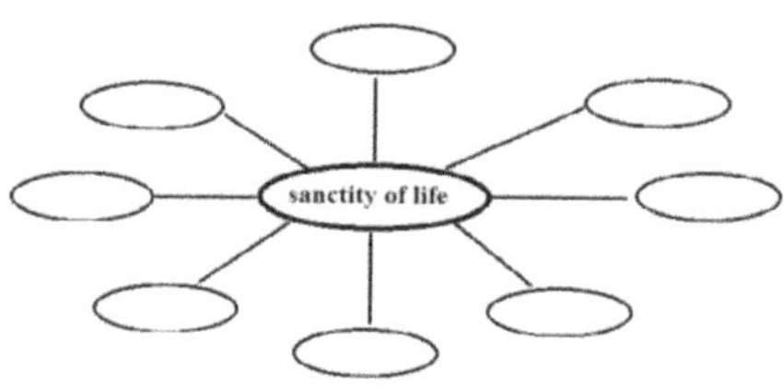

[33] One student quipped, "I feel like at the end of the year, my mind is going to be blown," prompting my response, "Hopefully, your brain is blown in some way every day, or close to it."

Students are asked to document various issues related to the Biblical concept of the sanctity of life. When completed, their Biblical concept map may look like this:

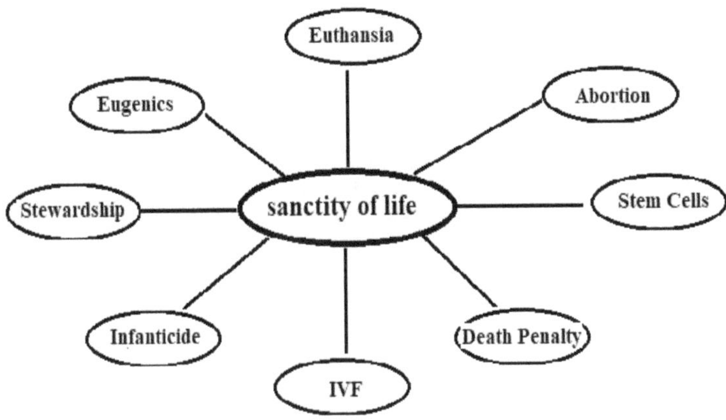

Mapping and connecting Biblical concepts with relatable topics, provides students a visual representation of how their worldview influences how they live in the world. Other Biblical concepts mapped include our bodies being the temple of God, one flesh (sexuality), and being made in the image of God.

Falling asleep in Applied is difficult when these are the issues we deal with daily.

Intermission 1:
A Nation in Crisis
Spiritual VIPs

Discussing God's existence and the Christian worldview plays a critical role in how we view others and ourselves. Christ's death and resurrection changes our perspective because we start with His work as opposed to ours. During our conversation on God's existence and worldviews, students are reminded they are VIPs.

Who would not want to be a VIP? Seeing many students who view themselves with no value and purpose, I have concluded that we are in crisis mode on this score.

Applied's VIP conversation is needed.

Young men and women (and adults) are lost. Even Christians have been convinced we are only evolved animals created to chase stacks of cash, buy fast cars and big homes, and get the latest fix. Our attempts at being very important people in the eyes our family, friends and the virtual world have failed and with great cost.

Atheism proclaims humans are the result of an improbable chance cosmic expansion of the universe. Value is based on external applications of self or worldly standards. We will never be enough, not only for ourselves but for others. Humans will always let others down. Enough will never be enough. There will always be more to gain and more to lose. Some try to buy their own value, whether it be with cash, their bodies, or at the expense of others. Scrutinizing themselves on social media and having parents apply unnecessary pressure, most young men and women do not view themselves in a favorable light. We do not matter because we are only matter.

Christ has a different perspective on our value. Christ's work at the cross gives a non-traditional VIP status. Instead of viewing VIP as "very important person," Applied views it as "value, identity and purpose." Christ forever changes all three.

If God does exist and God is responsible for life, and Jesus is God, then Jesus, the creator of the entire universe, died for you. One drop of His holy blood on the cross is more valuable than everything in the world combined.[34]

External standards from family or friends cannot compare to Christ's blood. As Christians, *His value* as Savior has been given to us. Alone, we stand as condemned worthless sinners. Christ's work on the

[34] 1 Corinthians 6:19-20

cross reconciles us to the Father. When He looks towards us in judgment, He does not see our sin, but instead the sacrifice of His son. He sees the holy, redemptive work of Christ, whose blood is far more valuable than that of condemned sinners. Attempts to find our own value on our own terms and create our own identity *ex nihilo* has left us broken.

Growing up, I was an athlete. Identity was found in humiliating my opponent, who were often my friends. Humility was not my forte, nor were academics. Placing our identity in earthly titles leaves us at risk of insecurities; insecurities that later need to be filled. One day, our GPA and amazing athletic ability fail to matter. Hooking up with girls no longer gains social status. Identifying as a jock, stud, athlete, or academic are quickly replaced with being a mother, father, employee, or employer.

But again, these extrinsic titles are placed on us by society. They change as our context changes. Running up and down the soccer field or basketball court does not happen like it used to after the age of thirty-five. What happens when your identity can no longer be fulfilled? Who are you then? What do you become? How do you fill your insecurities of no longer being who you once were; or who your parents want you to be?

Christ has a different perspective on our identity. A perspective that begins at the cross. His death acts as a substitute for the punishment we earned. We were once sinners, separated and alienated from God, in Christ,

> You are a chosen people, a royal priesthood, a holy nation, God's special possession, that you may declare the praises of Him who called you out of darkness into His wonderful light. Once you were not a people, but now you are the people of God; once you had not received mercy, but now you have received mercy.[35]

At the cross, the Father sees the identity of Christ given to us at our baptism, not our identity as sinners. Christ's divine value and identity is applied to us, so that our identity as sinners is not held against us. Searching for our own value and identity leaves us struggling to find a definitive purpose. The number of students who "do not know what they are doing with their lives" is staggering. Directionless autonomy leads them searching for popularity, fame, fortune, social status, and

---

[35] 1 Peter 2:9-10

financial stability. These are all deep voids which will never be filled. In the process, they hurt themselves and others.

Christ has a different perspective on our purpose, one that begins at the cross and moves forward from the cross:

> Jesus replied: "Love the Lord your God with all your heart and with all your soul and with all your mind.' This is the first and greatest commandment. And the second is like it: 'Love your neighbor as yourself.' All the Law and the Prophets hang on these two commandments."[36]

> Therefore go and make disciples of all nations, baptizing them in the name of the Father and of the Son and of the Holy Spirit, and teaching them to obey everything I have commanded you.[37]

Christ's purpose was redeeming and restoring man to the Father. Our purpose is to share this redemptive work with others. Christ's work on the cross transformed us from ugly sinners into glorified saints. We are His VIPs because of *His* very important propitiation on the cross.

Compare our value, identity, and purpose of Christ to a secular worldview.

Worldview Question 1: God does not exist and therefore,
Worldview Question 2: There is no spiritual realm or design, therefore,
Worldview Question 3: Humans are not redeemed valuable children of God, but evolved apes,
Worldview Question 4: Waiting to die, be buried and rot into nothingness.
Worldview Question 5: In the meantime, we grow in the knowledge of ourselves,
Worldview Question 6: Doing what we want and creating whatever identity we like
Worldview Question 7: with whatever purpose you desire, in hopes it helps society.

---

[36] Matthew 22:37-39
[37] Matthew 28:19-20

Christian Worldview	Atheistic Worldview
1 Peter 2:9: You are a chosen people, a royal priesthood, a holy nation, God's special possession, that you may declare the praises of him who called you out of darkness into His wonderful light. Once you were not a people, but now you are the people of God; once you had not received mercy, but now you have received mercy	In a universe of electrons and selfish genes, blind physical forces and genetic replication, some people are going to get hurt, other people are going to get lucky, and you won't find any rhyme or reason in it, nor any justice. The universe that we observe has precisely the properties we should expect if there is, at bottom, no design, no purpose, no evil, no good, nothing but pitiless indifference

Where can one's intrinsic value, identity, and purpose be found in the atheistic worldview? Rejecting God, society's aggressive shift towards embracing secularism, has left us in a crisis. Secular answers to life are subjective and vacant of eternal substance, almost by definition. A Christian worldview coherently answers each question because Christ himself is the answer.

Belonging to the Lord and being His VIP influences how we view life. Either we are valuable redeemed humans worthy of being protected or we are not. That is the lead into our next unit where we *apply* our worldview to the Biblical concept of the sanctity of life.

Chapter 6

Worldview Application

Life Issues: Abortion

Having identified our worldview, it is time to apply it to specific moral, ethical and spiritual issues of the world. In my earlier years of teaching, my transitions from one unit to the next were not smooth. Even now, there are times when the current unit does not directly connect to the previous one. However, that is not the case when talking about the sanctity of life.

Transitioning from examining the question of God's existence to applying our newly identified worldview to life issues is easy. There are significant implications if we have determined that God does actually exist. There is no greater example than abortion.

Every year, the abortion conversation begins by providing students seven scenarios that end with the question, "Would you consider recommending abortion in this situation?"

Applied's seating chart is chosen on purpose. Male students will be partnered with female students knowing that their perspectives may differ because of their gender. I already know that some support abortion, Christians included. At this stage of the conversation their reasoning behind their conclusion and ability to communicate with their classmate is priority. Soon they will be headed off to college where civil communication is vital even if it is not always practiced. Ben Shapiro's "Facts do not care about your feelings," is spot on.

After listening to individual reasoning for a few minutes, scenarios are then discussed.

One situation resides in the unknown future of the child in the womb. Imagine you and your future spouse hear your doctor speak these words, "medically speaking, the child has no real hope, we believe that you should have an abortion." This scenario seems unrealistic for most teenagers, but it is a reality for far too many later in life.

One scenario places the abortion dilemma in the lap of a high school student who is contemplating an abortion. More often than not, students are more interested in challenging the school's policy of asking unwed mothers and fathers to withdraw while they work through the pregnancy. Considering that most students have not read the policy and they are reacting on emotions and not knowledge, I read the policy to the class.[38] Hearing the policy puts most students at ease. Abortion is our focus though, not school policy.

When the initial days of conversation simmer down, each student is provided a photocopy of their biology textbook titled, "Properties of Life." Instructions include read the handout as well as applying the properties of life to the living entity inside a woman. Once they have completed their reading assignment, they are partnered up to discuss their applications. Five minutes are provided to make a mock conversation between a pro-life and pro-choice student. At the heart (pun intended) of this conversation are the seven properties of life.

Imagine you are sitting in your dorm room and your roommate notices you have a cross on your desk. She asks you, "You are a Christian? You oppose abortion?" With a tone of hesitancy, you reply, "Yes. Would you like to know my reasoning?"

Students can be put on the spot at any time. Little do they know that their dorm room conversation which may or may not happen is moments away from happening in Room 101 as the circle of death is resurrected: "Leave two desks in the middle and circle the other desks around those two. I will need two volunteers to read their scripted conversation in front of the rest of the class." Stomachs drop. Faces turn red. Palms are sweaty, knees weak, arms are heavy. Mom's spaghetti.[39]

Rather anti-climactic, but the buildup is killer. Each partnership reads their script for less than minute. Sometimes, they verbalize the main point within seconds of beginning. Partnership after partnership, a pattern begins to form. Remember, students were forced to include an application of the properties of life in their conversations. There is one major point being made with these universal properties of life: That which is growing inside of the woman is alive, from conception. This basic fact contradicts a position held by some who support abortion. Science does not let them off the hook.[40] Common sense and proven science demonstrates the human life is alive. If it was not alive, there would not be anything to abort. The entire intent of an abortion is to kill that which is alive!

Our common sensical, science-driven reasoning, continues by further addressing the nature of the entity living inside of the woman.

---

[38] I included this point to demonstrate students are expected to collect data and information when making decisions, as opposed to relying on emotionalism.

[39] One of my many cultural references to keep the students on their toes, and sometimes, smiling. Thank you, Eminem, for this gem that keeps on giving.

[40] I am pleased to see so many states supporting heartbeat bills, which protects the obvious, living, human life inside of a woman.

Pro-Abortion: It is only a zygote, blastocyst, or fetus.
Pro-Life response: What kind of zygote, blastocyst, or fetus, is it? Is it an elephant? Is it a dog fetus? What kind of DNA does it have?
Pro-Abortion: Human
Pro-Life response: Therefore, inside of the woman is a living human life.

Misogyny, anger, or hostility are not influencing the conversation of the position of the Christian. Science, *not religion* answers the questions above.

At this point of the year, I have demonstrated that I want students to grow and learn. It becomes clear I am willing to listen to questions and concerns. For the most part, students trust my guidance and approach which helps when talking about an emotionally charged topic such as abortion. My tone is not sardonic or demeaning, instead, my words are spoken with grace.

Often, students are the ones observing that the fetus, blastocyst or whatever, has human DNA and is therefore, a human. Students acknowledge that inside of a pregnant woman is a living human life. Denying such would be denying basic science.[41]

Pro-Abortion: It is my body.
Pro-Life: The living human inside of the woman has its own DNA, correct?
Pro-Abortion: Of course.
Pro-Life: And if it (the child) has its own human DNA, its own brain, heart, and organs, it has its own body.

Another human body lives inside of the woman. Should that innocent human life that has its own human body be protected?

Attempting to skirt this line of reasoning, some students look for a different argument to gain the upper hand in the conversation. One common assertion is that "It's just a parasite." When this is the

---

[41] The reason this is contentious boils down to a logical fallacy called 'equivocation.' The pro-abortionist is alternating between the use of the word 'human' as an adjective and as a noun. 'Fetus' is a noun; in the phrase 'human fetus' the word 'human' is being used to modify the word 'fetus.' The word 'fetus' refers to a stage of *development* of an entity and does not by itself tell us what kind of creature it is—that is what the adjective provides us! This equivocation surfaces in other lines of argument, too, like for example when the pro-abortion demands to know if a human skin cell should be given 'human rights.' But a human skin cell is not a human. In this case, the word 'human' is telling us what kind of skin cell it is. No one believes a skin cell is *a human*. But a human (adjective) fetus (noun) *is* a human (noun).

happens, I walk over to the binder sitting on my desk and grab a copy of Thomas L. Johnson's article, "Why the Embryo or Fetus is Not a Parasite."[42] Without missing a beat, I hand the piece of paper over to the questioning student and let them read his explanation. One time, a student who read the article responded, "Well, there's that," as he returned the handout.

Our first step in the abortion conversation is to address the obvious: Inside of the woman is a living human life. Someone can call that life whatever they want, but it does not change the scientific fact that it is a human life. Even calling it a clump of cells does not solve the dilemma. They are living, *human* cells with their own DNA. In case you were confused, to anyone reading this is also a clump of cells, just further developed than the cells forming in the woman and no longer inside the woman. Does that mean the reader is not a human?

Step one completed. Step two calls upon prior implications of asserting God's existence, His nature, and a moral law which assumes human life carries intrinsic value and worth.

Ray Comfort's popular "180" video, is viewed.[43] Comfort begins by interviewing an array of men and women. Conversations begin with Comfort asking participants their views on the Holocaust. Exceptions aside, those interviewed generally agree that Hitler's holocaust was evil. Innocent life should be protected is the prevailing sentiment.

Having set his interviewees up with a reasonable line of questioning, Comfort blindsides his subjects with a heavy question, "What do you think about abortion?" Wow. Moments ago, they were supporting the sanctity of life and now they find themselves in the position of trying to justify the destruction of innocent human life.

As it is common today, many end up contradicting themselves as Comfort continues his questioning. The usual justifications such as "Quality of life" and "It's not my choice" are echoed. The damage is done, though, as Comfort's approach illuminated the inconsistency of their position. Some of those who were interviewed changed their minds on abortion because innocent human life ought to be protected. There were others who were too entrenched in their position to contemplate valid reasoning.

Comfort's "180" video is an opportunity to evaluate the value of a human's life. If it was wrong to murder defenseless Jews, why is it morally acceptable to murder defenseless children (or blastocyst, or fetus, etc.)?

---

[42] http://www.141.org/library/notparas.html
[43] https://www.livingwaters.com/movie/180movie/

Our progression follows:

1. Science demonstrates that inside of the woman is a living human life, with its own body and DNA.
2. Innocent human life should be protected.
3. "It depends on the situation."

Challenging students who believe the situation determines abortion's acceptability, infanticide is now introduced. This is a term that recently made international news when a politician (or two) voiced indirect support for the practice. On the whiteboard the most common justifications for abortion are documented:

1. It will ruin my life
2. I plan on going to college
3. Only women can speak about abortion.[44]
4. I cannot financially take care of a child (notice the admission that it is in fact, a child)
5. I am not mentally or emotionally prepared to have a child
6. If the mother's life is in jeopardy
7. It's not a human life until it is viable
8. The woman was raped

In what context is it acceptable to murder an innocent human life?

Here is our scenario: A woman ends up pregnant and carries her child to term. She births the child but then loses her job and is no longer able to financially care for her child. Does this warrant infanticide, the killing of an infant? Does a parent's financial situation make the human life less valuable?

Take two children and place them next to each other. One set of parents has $10,000 in their bank account. The other set has $100,000. Which child has more value?

Contemplate another scenario where a mother carries her child to term, but due to Postpartum PTSD struggles to take care of her child. Has the value of the innocent[45] child changed because the mother's mental and emotional state has changed? Does this warrant infanticide?

What about abortion? Does an innocent child's value decrease because of the mother's mental and emotional stress? No. A human life's value is not dependent on external situations.

---

[44] Hardly a reasonable conclusion considering that the supreme court that decided abortion was acceptable consisted of men.

[45] The use of the word 'innocent' is important, as will become more evident in the next chapter.

Perhaps one of the most common arguments supporting abortion is viability. The idea is that, if a child is born prematurely, say, before 24 weeks, the child is not viable—that is, she is not capable of living or being kept alive. After 24 weeks, the child is considered viable and therefore is mostly protected by state laws (although, the political shift is on to normalize abortion up to birth and maybe beyond.[46])

After five days, five weeks, five months, or five years, *the life is still a human life*. Conceding the life expectancy of a premature birth at 10 weeks is not promising, it is still a living human child, with its own body. A premature birth at 34 weeks is still a living human child. This is again, scientific fact. As medical technology becomes more advanced, the age of viability changes. Internet searches furnish multiple examples of children born earlier than 24 weeks who have survived.

Scientist are working on creating artificial wombs and embryos in the laboratory.[47] [48] If scientists can create artificial wombs and sustain life at the earliest stages, the pro-abortionist argument from viability goes out the window.

Up this point of the conversation, we have not cited any Scripture or made any references to God. Nor do we have to, as the argument has been rooted in scientific fact. Some secular humanists who oppose abortion agree.[49] Students will tell you that as soon as you bring God into the conversation, people will ignore your voice.

Scripture, though, is straightforward, "Thou shalt not murder," (Exodus 20:13). There is no point within Christian Scripture where murdering innocent human life is justified. Scripture seeks to protect *innocent* human life.

Finally, we review the position by recalling our answer to worldview question three, "What is a human being?" Is a human life only an evolved animal destined for the grave? Or, is a human life made in the image of God? If God is responsible for human life, and human life has been made in the image of God, then innocent human life should be protected because it bears the image of God Himself. Asserting God's existence has significant implications, implications that may just happen to save a child's life if incorporated into someone's worldview.

---

[46] At the time of writing, Alabama passed a law declaring abortion illegal. Other states are following suit.

[47] https://www.ncbi.nlm.nih.gov/pmc/articles/PMC6252373/

[48] https://www.nature.com/articles/s41586-018-0051-0

[49] http://www.prolifehumanists.org/

What about rape? Earlier in *Applied Christianity* we made it clear that rape is vile and detestable. But does the situation of rape change our position on abortion? Answering a question with a question, "Does the woman being raped devalue the life of the child?"

Restating the question: Does the innocent child's intrinsic value lessen because the circumstances of his arrival in the world (at conception) were gross and detestable? Of course not.

Everyone can agree that rape should never happen but abortions via rape are the exception and not the norm. The pro-abortion Guttmacher Institute notes that less than <0.5 percent of abortions were related to rape. Of the thirteen reasons respondents provided for having an abortion, rape was tied for ninth.[50]

When we speak of the "sanctity of life," this is what we mean: God, the creator of the universe has made man and woman in His image. The destruction of innocent human life in the context of abortion should not be supported.

Attempting to use emotional argumentation, students challenge, "Mr. Horvath, what if your wife was going to die? Then what?" Students are again using an exception to justify legalizing abortion.[51] God, the creator of the universe has made man and woman in His image. The destruction of innocent human life, in the context of abortion should not be supported. "That sounds like a cop out, Mr. Horvath." To respond, I defer to my wife's stance when the question was posed to her; "The child lives."[52]

Society has decided that a woman's right to choose is more important than a child's right to life. Christians, however, ought to defend innocent human life and oppose its destruction by voting appropriately, peacefully protesting, prayer, or courageously defending innocent life when the conversation arises.

Our heavenly citizenship ought to trump our earthly citizenship.[53]

---

[50] https://www.guttmacher.org/sites/default/files/pdfs/tables/370305/3711005t3.pdf

[51] They are repeating what secular society has fed them.

[52] https://www.dublindeclaration.com/ "As experienced practitioners and researchers in obstetrics and gynecology, we affirm that direct abortion – the purposeful destruction of the unborn child – is not medically necessary to save the life of a woman. We uphold that there is a fundamental difference between abortion, and necessary medical treatments that are carried out to save the life of the mother, even if such treatment results in the loss of life of her unborn child. We confirm that the prohibition of abortion does not affect, in any way, the availability of optimal care to pregnant women."

[53] If the Supreme Court were to overrule Roe v. Wade in the future, abortion will not be declared illegal across the nation. The consequence of the court overturning Roe v. Wade would be that each state would be responsible for its own abortion laws. This aligns with the 10th Amendment of the Constitution of the United States. The power would be in the hands of the people and not the federal government.

Navigating the abortion topic can be difficult and intense. No doubt there are students who know or will know someone who has had an abortion. Christians must respond with gentleness, respect, compassion, humility, and love, and not condemnation. In class, students are encouraged to make themselves available to anyone who comes to them laden with guilt or shame for having an abortion. One might expect a woman who regrets their choice to shed tears. Comforting with a soft embrace, if permitted, is encouraged. Students are told, depending on the context, reading Romans 8:1-2 may be appropriate, with a strong emphasis on the word, "no."

> Therefore, there is now no condemnation for those who are in Christ Jesus, because through Christ Jesus the law of the Spirit who gives life has set you free from the law of sin and death.

Chapter 7

Life Issues: IVF, Euthanasia, Stem Cell Research, Capital Punishment

IVF

Bloom's Taxonomy and The Foundation for Critical Thinking's elements of thoughts are critical resources used in Applied.[54] Reliance on factual data and information to make informed decisions is lacking in the 21st century, and society seems content to accept ignorance. Applied refuses to allow students to reside in a lack of knowledge. You better know your reasoning behind making a conclusion! Recognizing that abortion is an emotionally charged topic does not change the common-sense fact that inside of the woman is a living human which deserves to be protected from conception to natural death. With the abortion conversation fresh in our mind, students are given a new scenario, that according to statistics, will be a reality for fifteen percent of couples:[55]

> Due to a variety of reasons, you and your spouse are not able to naturally conceive.

Using their cellphones, students research various fertility methods available to solve their problem. One possible method is In Vitro Fertilization (IVF). Having briefly researched IVF, most students support the concept of IVF. Why not? It seems like a viable option. Birthing their own biological child is important to many families and this is not lost in the conversation.

Our concern lies with the ethical and theological dilemma. As researched by students, IVF requires the creation of multiple embryos. Let us consider the implications of that fact.

Being the mathematical genius that I am, I use nine embryos for our in-class discussion. Jack and Jill want one child. Three embryos are implanted into the woman's uterus. With a success rate of less than 40 percent, the remaining six embryos are frozen for later use if needed. True to form, the first three failed. Three more embryos are implanted, and the parents wait in anticipation. Surprise, twins.[56]

But, what do we do with the remaining three frozen embryos?

---

[54] https://www.criticalthinking.org/

[55] https://www.mayoclinic.org/diseases-conditions/male-infertility/symptoms-causes/syc-20374773

[56] Two parents with two children requires man to man defense.

1. We can keep the embryos frozen for later use if we want another child
2. We can donate the embryos to science
3. We can discard the embryos altogether
4. We can place the embryos up for embryo adoption[57]

Our scenario becomes more complicated when we draw upon our previous abortion conversation. Science is clear, at conception, new human life is created. God is responsible for the creation of this new human life which has been made in His image. Staying true to our convictions that innocent human life should be protected, options one, two and three are off the table. If the embryo is a human life, of which it is, why would a Christian be in favor of freezing human life? Options two and three require the complete destruction of innocent human life.

One of the most common questions received every year is, "Why do so many people care about what Christians believe?"

Christianity makes bold claims that impact every area of life. For the hostile skeptic, Christians are hateful misogynist (because they oppose abortion) and bigoted obstacles preventing the progression of society.

Worldview question seven from the previous chapter asked, "What is the meaning of human history?" At the same time the Christian is interested in advancing two kingdoms, the hostile secularist is only interested in advancing one. Religion, you see, is a cancer and a curse that needs to be destroyed. It is, after all, the cause of all wars in history! Get rid of religion and wars will no longer happen.

Secularists that make that allegation will be disappointed to discover that religion is the cause of less than seven percent of recorded wars.[58]

Although IVF promises an alternative to those unable to conceive, Christians are concerned with freezing and destroying innocent human life, even in its earliest embryonic stage. This idea is absurd to secularists who believe religion is harmful to the progressive advancement of society. Whereas Christians are under the law of God, secular individuals want freedom *from* God. From their point of view if religion is abolished, freedom reigns and society is free to advance anywhere it chooses to whatever extent it desires (see stem cell research as one example).

---

[57] https://www.embryodonation.org/adoption/ Considered by some to be a viable option for individuals looking to save lives.

[58] Charles Phillips and Alan Axelrod, *The Encyclopedia of Wars*

What is a Christian to do if they cannot conceive? Despite the low success rate and high cost, some would recommend using only one embryo per IVF cycle. Dice are still being rolled, but at the very least, extra embryos are not being created with the intent of them being destroyed or frozen.

I am in no way condemning anyone who has used IVF. I know the realities of life. Graduates will be infertile. Doctors will offer multiple options for consideration. Being pro-life extends beyond the womb and fostering and adopting children become alternatives to those hesitant to use IVF for moral reasons.

Stem Cell Research

Another scenario is presented:

> The doctors have told you that your child (in or out of womb) has a severe medical issue that likely can be resolved using stem cells.

Prior conversations on God's existence, worldview question three, abortion, and IVF, influence student conclusions on stem cell research: innocent human life ought to be protected, not destroyed in research.

Reinforcing their independent conclusion, students are shown a DVD titled, "A Catholic View: The Science of Stem Cells." Finding Cures and Protecting Life.[59] The difference between adult and embryonic stem cells is thoroughly explained, with one of the major differences being the location from which the cells are cultivated.

Christians do not oppose using stem cells taken from bone marrow or amniotic fluid (adult stem cells). Objection is found in the destruction of human embryos (embryonic cells) as the cells are removed.

Saving your child from a debilitating disease is the first choice of any parent; but if saving your child results in the death of another human life, is it worth it? Does destroying an embryo for research align with your Christian worldview that innocent life bearing God's image should be protected?

Secular critics of Christianity here again see an opportunity to demonize Christians. In their view, the beliefs of Christians are hindering society's advancement by declaring an embryo a human life worthy of protection.

However, Christians are not opposed to scientific research and

---

[59] Available at https://www.youtube.com/watch?v=DUvsK2SCVdk

advancing man's knowledge so long as it does not compromise God's Kingdom.

These are not merely hypothetical scenarios. Real world examples of Christians wading through such issues abound.

One example is Christian apologist and author Anthony Horvath. After medical tests revealed his daughter had spina bifida,[60] the doctors encouraged him and his wife to abort their daughter, saying her life would be of low quality and filled with suffering. Or, so they said. They suggested that their unborn daughter was not worth the mental, emotional, physical, and financial investment. She would never walk. Or, so they said.

Never mind the suggestion of abortion and dismissiveness of innocent human life, why did doctors believe they were able to judge the quality of life for a child *not their own?* Even today, people believe that children with Down Syndrome should be aborted. Iceland has all but removed Down Syndrome via prenatal test and subsequent abortions.

Today, Anthony's daughter, restricted in movement, walks with a walker, and exudes more joy than most grown adults ever will, doctors included.[61]

Anthony and his wife were presented with the 'worst case scenario' and asked to make their decision based on that possibility, rather than the numerous other possibilities that existed. The worst-case scenario did not unfold. However, even if it had, it would not have meant the doctors were right. For the Christian, the 'quality' of one's life is separate from the intrinsic *value* of one's life.

Euthanasia[62]

After discussing the earliest stages of life, we go to the other side of the life continuum and move into a conversation on euthanasia. Clint Eastwood's, *Million Dollar Baby* is the day's anticipatory set.

In the movie, Eastwood plays an older and stubborn boxing coach (Frankie Dunn). Maggie, an aspiring female boxer pesters Coach Dunn in hopes he will teach her how to box. Dunn refuses until Eddie (played by Morgan Freeman) convinces him otherwise. Maggie bobs and weaves her way into a fight for the world championship, only to get sucker punched from behind at the end of round three, causing her to fall. Unfortunately, Maggie's neck lands on a fallen stool meant for her

---

[60] Failure of the spine and spinal cord to form properly (www.mayoclinic.org)
[61] You can read about their decision and her story at http://wechoselife.com/
[62] Which comes from the Greek word, Euthanatos, which means, "good death."

to sit on between rounds. Within seconds, Maggie's life changes as she becomes a bedridden quadriplegic.

Students are asked to create a T-chart like the one below as they watch *Million Dollar Baby*:

Scene in the movie	Corresponding worldview question
Eastwood prays to God in church	WV Q1: Eastwood believes in God's existence
Eastwood struggles with whether or not to euthanize Maggie	WV Q6: Is it moraly and spiritually wrong
Maggie sees no reason to live anymore	WV Q7: A Christian's is to love God, love people, and share the Gospel, regardless of circumstances

For a few in the classroom, watching may be an intense and emotional experience. Some students have already experienced seeing a loved one on life support or in hospice. They can relate to both Maggie and Coach Dunn. Our goal is not to pull on emotional strings, or even to focus on end of life decisions (although covered). Instead, Maggie's situation is used to introduce stewardship in the context of the sanctity of life.

We are not watching the movie for the sake of watching the movie. Important questions are asked, such as, "How does our Christian worldview influence Maggie's unfortunate situation?" and, "How does Maggie's situation relate to your current existence as a high school student?" Important lessons are to be gleaned from Maggie's rise from a no-name boxer to a world champion contender with an abundance of fame and future.

Though Maggie cannot move, she is cognizant and communicating with Coach Dunn who has not abandoned her bedside since the accident. Maggie's inability to move makes her situation worse as bed sores require body parts to be amputated, prompting Maggie to make an impossible request of her coach.

From Maggie's perspective, *her life* was over. *Her time* was up. She had accomplished everything *she* wanted to accomplish. She had money, fame, and fortune. The world knew *Maggie's* name. Being paralyzed from the neck down took her glory away. Her career was over and from her perspective, so too was life and any meaning. Maggie asks her coach to euthanize her like her dad euthanized her dog growing up. Struggling with the decision and after consulting with a priest, Coach Dunn acquiesces and ends Maggie's life by supplying her body with an overload of adrenaline.

Eastwood's *Million Dollar Baby* ignores the legalities of euthanasia and dares the viewer to consider their own lives and end of life situations. Applied's focus follows suit, focusing not on Dunn's illegal actions, but more on Maggie herself and her attitude as they apply to the Christian worldview. What should we do with Maggie's attitude?

C.S. Lewis again offers insight via *The Screwtape Letters*. Let's see if the reader can relate Screwtape's advice to his nephew Wormwood to Maggie's situation.

> Men are not angered by mere misfortune but by misfortune conceived as injury. And the sense of injury depends on the feeling that a legitimate claim has been denied. The more claims on life, therefore, that your patient can be induced to make, the more often he will feel injured and, as a result, ill-tempered. Now you will have noticed that nothing throws him into a passion so easily as to find a tract of time which he reckoned on having at his own disposal unexpectedly taken from him
>
> We produce this sense of ownership not only by pride but by confusion. We teach them not to notice the different senses of the possessive pronoun — the finely graded differences that run from "my boots" through "my dog", "my servant", "my wife", "my father", "my master" and "my country", to "my God". They can be taught to reduce all these senses to that of "my boots", the "my" of ownership. Even in the nursery a child can be taught to mean by "my Teddy-bear" not the old imagined recipient of affection to whom it stands in a special relation (for that is what the Enemy will teach them to mean if we are not careful) but "the bear I can pull to pieces if I like".[63]

Screwtape Letter 21 is a favorite of many students. Brief conversations with their partners reveal the enormous applications and implications on student's lives. One student so liked the phrase, "Men are not angered by mere misfortune but by misfortune conceived as

[63] C.S. Lewis, *The Screwtape Letters*

injury," he committed the phrase to memory on his own volition. Why would men be angered by misfortune that personally does not hit home? Men are angered by misfortune they perceive as a personal insult to their life. Driving past a car accident is less bothersome unless you are involved in the accident. Ever drive past a driver who was pulled over by the cops for speeding, only to chuckle and thank the Good Lord you were not being pulled over? One could easily surmise your reaction would be different if the officer was asking for your driver's license and registration, especially if you did not believe you were speeding.

Situations that impact others often lack importance to us. Yet, if it impacts *us*, it can ruin *our* day. Lewis provides additional insight as to why petty daily nuisances are taken as personal offense,

> The more claims on life, therefore, that your patient can be induced to make, the more often he will feel injured and, as a result, ill-tempered.

Screwtape highlights common statements of ownership when he reminds Wormwood that from birth, humans have been conditioned to take possession of "my boots" through "my dog", "my servant", "my wife", "my father", "my master" and "my country", to "my God". Each of those claims have their own consequence and implication. "Who stole my boots? I spent a lot of my money on those boots."

Greater than laying a claim to boots is laying claim to God when we expect God to behave and act according to our will as opposed to His.

Loved ones are lost every day to the wages of sin, which often gives birth to a common lament, "Why did God take *my* loved one? Didn't you know he belonged to me?" Or, "How come God did this to *me*?" We made a claim on our loved one and now we are angry at God for taking away *our* possession.[64] Anger and bitterness seeps in, and belief in God may be lost because God did not act in accordance to how we wanted *our* God to act.

Maggie claimed her life as her own. She answered worldview question seven, "What is the meaning of human history?" with, "Be the best boxer I could be gaining fame and fortune." Maggie's life was her own and so too was her purpose of hearing her name echo through stadiums.

Director Clint Eastwood went out of his way to place a cross around Maggie's neck during her last days. Despite this profession of faith,

[64] A justifiable human reaction. Job, Joseph, Paul, and Moses were not joyfully exuberant as they suffered. I'm not blaming or condemning individuals for being angry at God.

Maggie failed to see the irony of wearing a cross. When we profess Christ as our savior based on His work on the cross, we confess Him as Lord and not ourselves. We belong to the Lord:

> The earth is the LORD's, and everything in it, the world, and all who live in it; for he founded it on the seas and established it on the waters.[65]

> For none of us lives for ourselves alone, and none of us dies for ourselves alone. If we live, we live for the Lord; and if we die, we die for the Lord. So, whether we live or die, we belong to the Lord. For this very reason, Christ died and returned to life so that he might be the Lord of both the dead and the living.[66]

The truth is, we do *not* belong to ourselves. Our parents do *not* belong to us. Our children are *not* our children, but they are the *Lord's*.

Notice the stark contrast between the Christian worldview and the secular worldview. Christian's bow in humility recognizing their place next to the King of Kings and submit to His Lordship. In the secular worldview, we are our own gods making our own decisions and truth. "Who are you to judge me?" is often shouted by those whose choices are being questioned.

Christian theology teaches that we are God's stewards.

One definition of stewardship is, "the careful and responsible management of something entrusted to one's care."[67] Christians manage the possessions entrusted to them by the Lord. For example, my children do not belong to me, they are the children entrusted to me by the Lord. My wife is not my wife, she is the wife entrusted to me by the Lord. Significant implications follow. If my children belong to the Lord, my responsibility is to lead them to the cross and not towards Hollywood fame and fortune. Mrs. Horvath belongs to the Lord and therefore, I am to love her as much as Christ loved the church (who belongs to Him).[68]

When addressing this concept with high school teenagers, I say, "Get your hands off her ("their" girlfriend). She does not belong to you; she belongs to the Lord." A perspective that begins with, "The earth is the Lord's and everything in it," changes a Christian's perspective on life forever.

---

[65] Psalm 24:1-2
[66] Romans 14:7-8
[67] https://www.merriam-webster.com
[68] Ephesians 5:25, "Husbands, love your wives, just as Christ loved the church and gave Himself up for her."

Second, Maggie's situation teaches us another important lesson that relates to our previous abortion conversation. Maggie's situation did not diminish her value, but it also did not change her God-given purpose.

> Teacher, which is the greatest commandment in the Law?" Jesus replied: "'Love the Lord your God with all your heart and with all your soul and with all your mind.' This is the first and greatest commandment. And the second is like it: 'Love your neighbor as yourself.[69]

Maggie may have had her leg amputated but having one less limb does not change her divine purpose. Paralyzed or not, our divine purpose remains true. Location does not change the innocent intrinsic value of a child in the womb, nor does location and ability change one's responsibility and opportunity of carrying out God's purpose.

Secular atheists who want to lord over their own life and live their own purpose find living for God an absurd idea, which is not a surprising conclusion considering Dawkins's accurate explanation of what atheism entails when taken to its logical end,

> The total amount of suffering per year in the natural world is beyond all decent contemplation. During the minute that it takes me to compose this sentence, thousands of animals are being eaten alive, many others are running for their lives, whimpering with fear, others are slowly being devoured from within by rasping parasites, thousands of all kinds are dying of starvation, thirst, and disease. It must be so. If there ever is a time of plenty, this very fact will automatically lead to an increase in the population until the natural state of starvation and misery is restored. In a universe of electrons and selfish genes, blind physical forces and genetic replication, some people are going to get hurt, other people are going to get lucky, and you won't find any rhyme or reason in it, nor any justice. The universe that we observe has precisely the properties we should expect if there is, at bottom, no design, no purpose, no evil, no good, nothing but pitiless indifference.[70]

When there is only pitiless indifference, it is not difficult to see why a secular atheist would support abortion, euthanasia, stem cell research, IVF, and other fertility treatments without exception.

---

[69] Matthew 22:36-40

[70] Richard Dawkins, *River Out of Eden,* page 133

America's secular culture encourages citizens to embrace a "My body, my choice," attitude, an attitude contrary to the Christian principle of stewardship. A woman's (or man's) body is not her body to do as she pleases. She belongs to the Lord. The Lord owns her (and him), she does not own the Lord.

More so, the living body in the womb, or laboratory waiting to be used for research, belongs not to the woman, or scientist, but to the Lord. And if we belong to the Lord, His purpose becomes our priority.

Capital Punishment (death penalty)

"Then why do Christians support the death penalty?"

Up to this point we have chosen our previous words on the sanctity of life *very carefully*. God answers the question in His Word,

> And for your lifeblood I will surely demand an accounting. I will demand an accounting from every animal. And from each human being, too, I will demand an accounting for the life of another human being. "Whoever sheds human blood, by humans shall their blood be shed; for in the image of God has God made mankind[71]

Why does a Christian support the death penalty? One obvious reason is that God's Word declares it acceptable. Why? Humans have been made in *His* image. Violating *His* image is reprehensible. So egregious is murder says the Lord, that those who murder a human, by a human shall their blood be shed. But what about protecting the sanctity of life?

The key distinction here is that the individual found guilty of murder is not innocent.[72] Scripture is loaded with references to protecting innocence.[73] Murderers are not innocent. Worse, the murderer violated both God's law and God's image, resulting in the ultimate punishment, death.

God's command needs to be viewed in its proper context. Cain killed Abel and was condemned to wander the earth, not death. Humanity continued to defile God's image to the point "The LORD regretted that He had made human beings on the earth, and His heart was deeply troubled."[74] God destroyed His creation with a massive

---

[71] Genesis 9:5-6.
[72] Purposefully used fifteen times in this chapter and thirteen in the previous chapter.
[73] Exodus 23:1-9 for example.
[74] Genesis 6:6

flood, saving eight individuals. After the flood waters receded, God blessed Noah and gives Him a moral law for the ages:[75]

> But you must not eat meat that has its lifeblood still in it. And for your lifeblood I will surely demand an accounting. I will demand an accounting from every animal. And from each human being, too, I will demand an accounting for the life of another human being. "Whoever sheds human blood, by humans shall their blood be shed; for in the image of God has God made mankind. As for you, be fruitful and increase in number; multiply on the earth and increase upon it.[76]

These words follow the flood but precede the Mosaic Law found within Scripture. God's command to protect innocent life and administer severe consequences to those who violate His law are included and put into practice in the later Mosaic law. God's protection of innocent life does not stop with the Old Testament, let alone Genesis 9:6. Scripture echoes the concept throughout.

One cannot argue that God was against hurting people in all contexts when many of His commands included death. In the context of stewardship, even the murderer belonged to the Lord and His wrath, not 21st century Americans. How would God carry out this wrath?

> But if you do wrong, be afraid, for rulers do not *bear the sword for no reason. They are God's servants, agents of wrath to bring punishment on the wrongdoer*. Therefore, it is necessary to submit to the authorities, not only because of possible punishment but also as a matter of conscience.[77] [Emphasis added]

Refuting the argument that we have no place to judge or execute God's wrath, His Word specifically says His own image bearers would be responsible for administering justice to those who murder others. Both Paul and Jesus recognize that the Father has given His creation the authority to administer His justice. Paul states that if he has done anything worthy of death, so be it (Acts 25:10-11).

Upon being questioned by Pilate, Jesus recognizes Pilate has the authority to crucify him, but only because the authority has been given from above (John 19:10-11).

---

[75] Referred to as a Noahide Law. See Dennis Prager's, *The Rational Bible: Genesis* for more information.

[76] Genesis 9:4-7

[77] Romans 13:3-5

Are innocent people put to death? Yes. It is for this reason Christians can in good conscience support organizations like the Innocence Project, which seeks to exonerate those incorrectly accused.[78]

Likewise, arguing for a moratorium on the death penalty is a worthy position. Christians have a responsibility to protect image bearers of God, even if they are in prison, or in the womb, or in the freezer, or in the laboratory, or after birth-up, until natural death. Precisely because innocent lives need to be fiercely protected, if one believes there are reasons a system or government might fail to ensure that it is the murderer that dies, and not the innocent, a Christian might seek another way.

Nonetheless, in principle at least, there is more than a Scriptural argument to be made for capital punishment, there is a mandate. Ironically and conversely, if you *don't* execute a murderer for taking an innocent life, you are *not* upholding the preciousness of each individual life, because you are diminishing the value of the innocent life that was taken.

So, whether you support capital punishment or, for practical purposes, do not support it, it is important to think carefully about your reasons and ground them in the Scriptures.

[78] https://www.innocenceproject.org/

Intermission 2

Maintaining a strong foundation in life is critical. Knowing who you are, what you believe in, why you believe what you believe, and why you are alive provides direction. Ignorance of self and why you do what you do often leads to destruction. When the wind blows, and the rains fall (Matthew 7:24-29), you may be blown away or drown.

Former Navy Seal Mark Divine agrees,

> The perpetual winds of pleasure blow you in one direction. The gusts of pain push you in another. The problem is this keeps you from living your ideal life. You're simply bouncing around. By defining your stand and purpose, you will be able to use them as an internal GPS. When the winds of pain and pleasure blow, you won't change course.[79]

God is a Christian's strong and impervious foundation. He is their Rock. He is the GPS. But if one's belief in God is lacking or one doubts His existence altogether, it is easier for the winds of pleasure and life to change one's course.

Discussing God's existence becomes the priority. It sets our foundation and begins to shape our worldview, which answers life's most important questions, which provides direction. Life's inevitable rains and furious winds cannot be avoided. Standing on the Rock gives us purpose, direction, and firm footing, even in life's storms.

Applied's progression in logical:

> God's Existence influences… (Unit 1)
> Your worldview influences life's most important questions. (Unit 2)
> Answers to life's most important questions allows you to address life's most important issues such as abortion, stem cell research, euthanasia, etc. (Unit 3)

These three units transition well from one to the next, providing important building blocks to the student's foundation. Just before CHRISTmas we start the process of adding more foundational bricks by discussing historical apologetics. Lutheran North is a Christian school where most of the students are Christian. Despite this, many

---

[79] Mark Divine, *The Way of the Seal: Think Like an Elite Warrior to Lead and Succeed*, page 14.

have unanswered questions about the Holy Scriptures.

1. Are the contents of the Scriptures historically reliable?
2. Who wrote the New Testament?
3. How much did the New Testament change from the 1st century to the 21st century?
4. When did Christianity begin? Did it evolve over time?
5. Do the Scriptures contradict?

Boring historical questions to some, but essential for all, and worthy of addressing in Applied. Second semester affords us the opportunity to apply our foundational bricks to topics relating to sanctification, sex, drugs, and tattoos. You cannot have a conversation on "What does the Bible says about..." if you cannot trust the Holy Scriptures.

Instead of moving from historical apologetics to issues of sanctification and back to historical apologetics, *Applied Christianity* will first walk through a historical analysis of Scripture as presented in Applied. Part four will address issues of sanctification which are sprinkled throughout the curriculum during the year. The reader is free to choose their own adventure, part three or part four.

Part III

Historical Christianity

Chapter 8

Gospel Authorship and Timing of the New Testament

Historical apologetics is another major focus of Applied. Apologetics stems from the Greek word, "apologia," which means to "make a defense." Paul exhorts his listeners 1 Peter 3:15 to give an 'apologia' for the Gospel:

> But in your hearts revere Christ as Lord. Always be prepared to give an answer to everyone who asks you to give the reason for the hope that you have. But do this with gentleness and respect.

Much of Paul's ministry consisted of defending Christ, the need for Christ, and Christ's resurrection. Despite this, some reject apologetics, believing its practitioners are attempting to replace the work of the Spirit and the power of the Word. Nothing could be further from the truth.

Paul recognized people doubted Jesus. Answering those questions and doing so with gentleness and respect was of paramount importance. Every Applied student has questions about their faith and its relationship to life. Answers abound within the Holy Scriptures. But if a student does not trust the Scriptures, then what? Prudency demands answering questions before sending students off to college where their worldview will be directly or indirectly challenged by professors, roommates and growing anti-Christian sentiment.[80]

Questioning students are provided data and information to assist in answering important questions, not to create faith, which is God's work. Ravi Zacharias's comment that sometimes you must go through the head to get to the heart is accurate. Our emphasis is on answering the students' own questions, not preparing students to fight with the secular establishment. Students have questions, I have answers.[81]

Social media has done intellectualism a great disservice. Most students find their news and "truth" from social media outlets. Assumptions are carried from the Internet into the classroom. Insisting on rational thinking and not emotionalism or popular tweets is reinforced ad nauseum.

---

[80] Within the last few years, multiple students have shared stories of professors being intolerant of the Christian worldview.

[81] Despite the critical nature of Christian apologetics, I believe that some of the greatest challenges to one's faith lie in the subtleties of life. These challenges are discussed in the following unit.

One such assumption assumes Christians commit intellectual suicide by believing in Jesus. While the Christian admits reliance on blind faith in certain (very limited) areas, God never expected His initial believers to operate on blind, ignorant faith. To the contrary, God Himself sought to give good reasons to trust Him and His word. A few examples follow:

1. God shows himself in the burning bush.
2. The plagues and God's deliverance of the Israelites
3. Moses brings water out of rock via God's work.
4. The parting of the sea during the exodus of the Israelites.
5. The flood.
6. Jesus healing the physical ailments of sick people in front of witnesses
7. Jesus showing His wounds to Doubting Thomas after His resurrection
8. The miracles carried out by the apostles gave testimony to the work of God.[82]
9. Resurrection of Christ.

Jesus walking down Jerusalem's Main Street shouting "I am God," would not have convinced many Jews. Literally anyone could do that. Healing a paralytic while claiming to be God would elicit different responses. Jesus backed up His words with physical manifestations of His deity for all to see. Time after time, God gave His people visible signs to verify His divine claim. Blind faith was not a role in God's initial deliverance of mankind (Old Testament or New).

Who wrote the Scriptures? When did they write the Scriptures? Can we trust the New Testament? Has it changed too much over time? Historical apologetics is not always an exciting unit for 12th graders looking to graduate, but the conversation is critical as we answer questions related to one the most important foundational bricks, God's Word.

Our chosen anticipatory set pits an imaginary Christian versus a skeptic. Partners are provided four prompts of which the skeptic takes the lead in challenging the Christian:

1. What makes you think Matthew, Mark, Luke, and John are the authors of the Gospels?
2. Why don't Matthew, Mark, and Luke reference the divinity of Jesus?

---

[82] Hebrews 2:1-4

3. How can you trust the New Testament, considering it was written more than thirty years after the life and death of Jesus?
4. The teachings of Christianity developed over hundreds of years. Why trust a story that is nothing more than a legendary tale?

We focus particularly on Christianity's origin and the underlying documentation. Students are provided a pie chart that is initially blank, but later filled with copious amounts of information to assist their research.[83] Labeled, "Data and Information," the most important part of the chart takes time to fill. Often, many Christians have zero pieces of data and information to answer the four accusations. When completed with our research, the number changes, signifying the individual progressed from ignorance to educated.

Challenge 1

Good reasons exist as to why Christians assign authorship to the four gospels. Responders are encouraged to answer questions with questions.

Skeptic: What makes you think Matthew, Mark, Luke, and John are the authors of the Gospels?
Christian: What makes you think they are not the authors of the Gospels?

In this instance, answering a question with a question brings to light the skeptic's own 'blind' faith. Skeptics of Christianity can often be found making blind accusations, assuming that since they heard the traditional authors aren't the real authors, it must be true. However, they did not do any research of their own to come to that conclusion. They are taking it on faith—in a tweet, for example. In exchanges such as the one above, they are expecting the Christian to provide evidence and documentation that they themselves didn't do for their own position. At minimum, that's unfair. However, it also might drive them to study the matter themselves, after which they might realize that the evidence is nothing like what they supposed.

Another example is when they accuse Scripture of contradicting itself. If met with such an accusation, a fair question of response can be offered, "Can you provide an example of a Biblical contradiction?"

[83] See appendix four.

Silence typically follows. Similar silence follows after asking skeptical individuals why they doubt the assigned authorship of the Gospels. What reasons do you have to doubt Matthew, Mark, Luke, and John are the Gospel authors?

This is not to say there are not reasonable questions to ask. Just as we are expecting the skeptic to bring to the table more than assertions, Christians should expect to do the same. Asking thoughtful questions is a good way to do that.

For example, one good question about the authorship of the Gospels is the curious lack of self-identification in them. It would have been nice if Matthew began his writing, "I am Matthew, I am writing this Gospel," but for a variety of reasons he chose not to. While this seems strange to us, this may very well have to do with our own modern-day cultural expectations when it comes to authorship. When we look back in time, it turns out that Matthew, and the other gospel authors, are not the only works of antiquity to not assign their name to their own work.[84]

What at first seems like a 'problem' ends up not being very worrisome at all. Popular and well-respected manuscript skeptic Bart Ehrman is not overly concerned with the lack of self-identification.[85]

Part of the answer to, "What makes us think these are the Gospel authors?" is we have no reason to doubt their authorship. History lacks any documentation challenging Gospel authorship. Let me restate that point: There are not any historical documents from the 1st, 2nd, or 3rd centuries (and beyond) that challenge the authorship of the Gospels. Instead, early Christian writings do ascribe Gospel authorship to Matthew, Mark, Luke, and John.

Papias, an apostolic father who was connected to the disciple John, identifies Matthew and Mark as the authors of two Gospels in his early 2nd century writing.[86] Irenaeus, in 180 AD, highlights the authorship of all four Gospels.[87]

Students remember from their sophomore theology classes that textual clues within Scripture can assist in identifying gospel authorship. One example of internal evidence for John's authorship is found in John 22:24, "This is the disciple who testifies to these things and who wrote them down. We know that his testimony is true." "This" disciple refers to the disciple whom Jesus loved, John.

---

[84] In the name of science and truth, Galen avoided placing his full name at the beginning of his books. https://www.encyclopedia.com

[85] https://ehrmanblog.org/

[86] Usually given the date AD 125

[87] *Against Heresies*

Christian apologist Lee Strobel argues that no one in the early centuries challenged gospel authorship, but also there would not be any motivation to lie about their authorship.[88] Matthew was a tax-collector, Luke was not even a direct eyewitness to Jesus. If the church was going to conspire against its people, they could have chosen more authoritative authors to make their lie stronger and more convincing.

In 125 AD, Papias records Matthew and Mark as two gospel authors. Was he lying? Yes? What historical documentation proves that assertion? Why was he lying? Was it a coverup? Excellent. Prove the assertion with historical documentation. Where are the manuscripts arguing differently?

If anything, if Matthew, Mark, Luke, and John were not the authors of the Gospels, you would think, looking to save their own lives, they would have written otherwise. Christians were not appreciated in the 1st century, nor in a position of power until the 4th century. Identifying oneself as an author of one of those blasphemous Christian documents would not have been the brightest idea.

Robust reasons allow us to trust Matthew, Mark, Luke, and John as the Gospel authors:

1. There are no evidence-based reasons to doubt Gospel authorship.
2. History lacks historical documentation suggesting alternative authorship.
3. What motivation would the church have for lying about Gospel authorship?
4. And if they were lying, why not choose more prominent individuals to bolster their case? For example, why not Jesus himself?
5. History lacks documentation from Matthew, Mark, Luke, and John rejecting authorship.
6. Textual clues within Scripture assist in identifying authorship despite the authors not providing them directly.
7. Historical writings do assign authorship to Matthew, Mark, Luke, and John.

These reasons, coupled together, offer a strong response to the question, "What makes you think Matthew, Mark, Luke, and John are the authors of the Gospels?"

---

[88] Author of *The Case for Christ* which, up to 2019, was a required textbook for Applied.

Challenge 2

Skeptic: Why don't Matthew, Mark, and Luke reference Jesus's divinity?
Christian: They do.

John's Gospel, the skeptic argues, is the only Gospel that refers to Jesus's divinity; and it was written after 90 AD, almost sixty years after the death of Jesus. Matthew, Mark, and Luke were written thirty years earlier than John's Gospel. Skeptics contend that those three Gospels do not contain claims or even hints of Jesus's divinity. Therefore, so goes their reasoning, the story of Christ was embellished because the later Gospel (John), is the only writing referring to Jesus's divinity.

This sounds convincing until one important detail is discovered: Matthew, Mark and Luke *do* refer to Jesus's divinity.

Mark's Gospel is widely considered the earliest Gospel of the four. Convinced by secular society, students often assume Christianity's teachings and beliefs evolved over centuries. Finding references to Jesus's divinity in the earliest Gospel would prove the assumption incorrect. Understanding Judaism and Jesus's culture provides necessary context. First century Jews knew their history and Scripture well. Jews cherished their faith, matching their verbal proclamation with action. Judaism was not something a Jew merely did; it was who they were.

> These commandments that I give you today are to be on your hearts. Impress them on your children. Talk about them when you sit at home and when you walk along the road, when you lie down and when you get up. Tie them as symbols on your hands and bind them on your foreheads. Write them on the doorframes of your houses and on your gates.[89]

Jesus makes a bold claim in Mark's Gospel, in fact, a divine claim: "For even the Son of Man did not come to be served, but to serve, and to give his life as a ransom for many," Mark 10:41-45.

An outsider, especially thousands of years removed, reads "Son of Man" as a statement of humanity and not divinity. Devout Jews would have known otherwise because meditating on Scripture was daily

[89] Deuteronomy 6:6-9. And to think, Christian schools across the country choose to not have their students memorize the Word of God.

practice. As such, that phrase would have immediately called to mind Daniel 7:13-14, which reads:

> In my vision at night I looked, and there before me was one like a son of man, coming with the clouds of heaven. He approached the Ancient of Days and was led into his presence. He was given authority, glory and sovereign power; all nations and peoples of every language worshiped him. His dominion is an everlasting dominion that will not pass away, and his kingdom is one that will never be destroyed.

The Jews, who took blasphemy very seriously, were therefore justified in their anger towards Jesus because calling oneself the "Son of Man" was tantamount to claiming to be divine.

Likewise, His claims of forgiving sins on His own authority (also included in Matthew, Mark, and Luke).[90] Israelites only accepted and worshipped one God, and Jesus was claiming He was the one "given authority, glory and sovereign power" and was worthy of worship by all "nations and peoples."

Remember, blasphemy was one of the reasons they nailed Jesus to the cross. Remember, too, that Mark's Gospel precedes John's Gospel. Jesus claims to be of divine origin and status in Mark's Gospel. Therefore, Jesus's divinity is not a theological development within Christianity but rather was present from its inception.

Challenge 3

Skeptic: How can you trust the New Testament, considering it was written more than thirty years after the life and death of Jesus?
Christian: Do *you* trust *any* history?

The idea behind this challenge is that the longer it takes for an event to be written down after it occurred, the less credible the document's account of the event. Skeptics attempt to discredit the New Testament by suggesting the gap between Jesus's life and writings about Him is too large. Challengers predominantly focus on the Gospels and not the rest of the New Testament. Addressing the argument, students are provided a prompt:

> If you were reading a book on the recent history of New York, which events might the author include?

---

[90] Matthew 9:1-3, Mark 2:1-12

Without exception, 9/11 is the most common answer. We then ask, "If the book said nothing about the tragedy of 9/11, what might we conclude about the book?" Numerous answers are given, with the most prominent being the conclusion that the book was most likely written before 9/11. New York's tragedy was such a monumental experience felt across the world, one would be shocked if a New York historian failed to mention the event.

Proceeding the first prompt is yet another that can be easily answered if students paid attention in 9th and 10th grade theology classes:

> How important was the Jewish temple to Judaism and its destruction in 70 AD?

Why is it that *no* New Testament writings include the temple's destruction, a monumental moment in Judaism that reverberates into modern history? Christianity flowed from Judaism, with Jesus being the fulfillment of messianic prophecy. Initial converts to Christianity were God-fearing, Jews who would have been impacted by its destruction.[91]

Acts, written by Luke, is a historical explanation of early Christianity in Jerusalem, yet the writing fails to mention the temple destruction, leading scholars to conclude that Acts and other New Testament writings were completed before 70 AD.

Traditional dating places Acts near 62 AD-64 AD. Chapters 7 through 24 detail the apostle Paul's ministry. He was *the man*.[92]

Prior to converting to Christianity, Paul dragged Christians out of their homes with the intent of sending converts to prison.[93] He even looked on, with approval, as Christians were stoned to death. After becoming a Christian, he traveled hundreds of miles preaching the Gospel of Christ. He was beaten, persecuted, and placed in prison. Paul had the full anti-Christian experience he once inflicted on Christians.

Near the end of Acts, Paul is under house arrest in Rome. In 64 AD, Rome was literally on fire. Instead of taking responsibility, Emperor Nero blamed Christians. Tacitus provides an account of Christians being used as used as illumination devices for his garden:

> In their very deaths they were made the subjects of sport: for they were covered with the hides of wild beasts, and worried to

---

[91] Much of Acts contains discussions on Judaism's place within Christianity.

[92] Lowercase "m." (A catch phrase reminding students Jesus is The Man)

[93] Acts 8:3

> death by dogs, or nailed to crosses, or set fire to, and when the day waned, burned to serve for the evening lights. Nero offered his own garden players for the spectacle, and exhibited a Circensian game, indiscriminately mingling with the common people in the dress of a charioteer, or else standing in his chariot. For this cause a feeling of compassion arose towards the sufferers, though guilty and deserving of exemplary capital punishment, because they seemed not to be cut off for the public good, but were victims of the ferocity of one man.[94]

Under house arrest, Paul, one of the premier Christians in the 1st century, continued to preach the Gospel. Yet, Acts not only fails to mention the temple's destruction, but also Paul's death and Nero's persecution of Christians in 64 AD. Why?

Scholars conclude Acts was written before the events above took place. Such reasoning confidently places Acts' composition earlier than 64 AD. Important for two reasons, Luke's introduction to Acts begins, "In my former book, Theophilus, I wrote about all that Jesus began to do and to teach until the day he was taken up to heaven, after giving instructions through the Holy Spirit to the apostles he had chosen."[95] Luke's Gospel addressed the same individual:

> Many have undertaken to draw up an account of the things that have been fulfilled among us, just as they were handed down to us by those who from the first were eyewitnesses and servants of the word. Since I myself have carefully investigated everything from the beginning, I too decided to write an orderly account for you, most excellent Theophilus, so that you may know the certainty of the things you have been taught.[96]

If Acts was written after Luke, and Acts was written before 64 AD, Luke's Gospel can be dated as being written before 63 AD. Mark and Matthew are widely accepted to have been before Luke, placing their composition before 63 AD. Simple inferences then drive us to believe that we can conclude that Matthew and Mark were also written before the fall of Jerusalem, in the mid to late 50s, possibly early 60s.

Jesus dies in 33 AD. Paul converts to Christianity a few years after the death of Jesus, leaving a gap of less than thirty years between the writings of the New Testament and the life of Jesus. Suggesting the

---

94 Tacitus, *Annals of History*

95 Acts 1:1-2

96 Luke 1:1-4

New Testament was written more than a century (or even 40 or 50 years) after the life of Jesus places one completely at odds with the evidence.

Skeptics and inquiring Christians may grant the New Testament's composition being less than thirty years after the life of Jesus but wonder if the content can be trusted. That depends on whether one is going to dismiss first and secondhand eyewitness testimony.

Mark recorded Peter's eyewitness testimony who himself declares, "For we did not follow cleverly devised stories when we told you about the coming of our Lord Jesus Christ in power, but we were eyewitnesses of his majesty."[97] Luke started his Gospel assuring Theophilus he "carefully investigated everything from the beginning" having received his material from eyewitnesses. If Mark and Luke were not direct eyewitnesses, how can we trust their words?

Answering a question with a question, "Why *can't* we trust their words?" Because they are in the Bible? And the Bible is to be dismissed without question? Is that your position?

Multiple points of consideration are worthy of discussion. First, the "Bible" is a larger collection of writings from individual authors, from various locations and at different times. That individual Scriptures were eventually codified into what we now call the "Bible" does not discredit their authenticity. Second, despite popular belief, the New Testament is rooted in history. There is a plethora of historical references found in the New Testament which can, and in many cases have been corroborated.

People would have us believe that the Jews who helped found Christianity created an unverifiable fairytale and managed to convert Jews (and Romans) who were looking for a verifiable messiah:

Jewish Conspirators: We have seen the messiah.
Jewish Skeptics: That's great, where is he?
Jewish Conspirators: Oh, he doesn't exist, the story is entirely fabricated. But you should give up thousands of years of Jewish history, heritage, and belief to convert.
Jewish Skeptics: Deal! We can't wait to be used as illumination devices by Nero for a fake, unverifiable, and concocted story.

Documentation of Hannibal's crossing the Alps to surprise the Romans provides a third response to the idea that Mark and Luke

[97] 2 Peter 1:16

cannot be trusted.[98]

Polybius and the Roman historian, Livy, are considered authoritative source material for Hannibal's maneuver. Mark this: neither Polybius nor Livy were eyewitnesses. Both seem to use the same source who may have been an eyewitness. Sound familiar? Polybius wrote about 70 years after the event,[99] whereas Livy wrote over 120 years later after Hannibal's crossing.

Here is what we know. Hannibal marched his army, through the Alps to surprise the Romans. Sources? Two non-eyewitnesses writing years later.

Mark's Gospel is rooted in Peter's eyewitness observations. Luke declares his intent was to carefully investigate the claims of Christianity for Theophilus. Both are using source material from within the same decades as the eyewitnesses.

For some reason, though, zero credibility will be given to the New Testament despite their written mathematical dominance compared to other ancient works. Less than thirty years is far superior to more than seventy years. Even if Livy and Polybius were both using earlier eyewitness testimony, so too were Mark and Luke, so what is the problem, exactly? Why hold the New Testament documents to a standard we won't hold other ancient documents? And conversely, if the New Testament documents meet or exceed the standards we have for other ancient documents, shouldn't we consider them at least as credible, if not more, than those documents?

After evaluating Hannibal's source material, we shift to Herodotus who I was introduced to indirectly by a study hall student asking for help on an assignment. Having not paid attention in high school, I was curious to learn about Herodotus.

Turns out, Herodotus is considered the "Father of History,"[100] because he was one of the first to "carefully investigate," before documenting his findings. What were his method and sources? Donald Lateiner includes in his introduction to Herodotus's work:[101]

> Herodotus names many sources, literary, documentary; oral, and material. Most of Herodotus' sources were certainly oral: individuals and groups with whom he spoke, such as descendants of the Spartans who died at Thermopylae, or

---

[98] https://www.livius.org/articles/person/hannibal-3-barca/hannibal-in-the-alps/

[99] https://www.britannica.com/biography/Polybius

[100] Cicero, *On the Laws*

[101] Herodotus, *The Histories*, Introduction notes and revisions by Donald Lateiner; translated by G.C. Macaulay

> acquaintances of participants in battle at Marathon…In between come eyewitness reports, an invaluable but slippery source for past events.

Translation? Herodotus was relying on information other than his own. Many of his sources were oral, descendants of Spartans or even acquaintances of participants in Thermoplyai or Marathon.

Matthew and John were eyewitnesses of the life of Christ. Mark, who was alive at the time of Peter, recorded Peter's experiences. Luke, who would have been born shortly during or after the life of Jesus (like Herodotus growing up fifteen years after the start of the Persian wars) wrote,

> Many have undertaken to draw up an account of the things that have been fulfilled among us, just as they were handed down to us by those who from the first were eyewitnesses and servants of the word. With this in mind, since I myself have carefully investigated everything from the beginning, I too decided to write an orderly account for you[102]

Herodotus's work, though sketchy at times, is generally accepted, and his methods applauded. His sources were mostly oral tradition and antiquated. And yet, though documented and rooted in eyewitness testimony, the New Testament is disqualified as authentic despite having a better historical record!

Questioning the New Testament does not offend me. Question all you want, but do not apply a double standard, accepting one over the other simply because the other document is "The Bible."

Suggesting the writings of the New Testament occurred ten or twenty years after the dates provided on previous pages, scholars who are critical of the New Testament disagree with the conclusions above. Internet skeptics who believe themselves to be intellectuals buy into a different line of thinking, arguing the New Testament was not written until hundreds of years after the life and death of Jesus. Refutation is easy.

Christians in the first part of the first century shared the Gospel message, converting many. First and second century believers of Christianity were plentiful. Some of these very early converts were Polycarp, Papias, and Ignatius, who wrote about their beliefs, thus giving us an early window into the content of Christianity at the time. Within their writings are references to Christian practices and New

---

[102] Luke 1:1-4

Testament writings. A simple timeline helps illustrate the point:

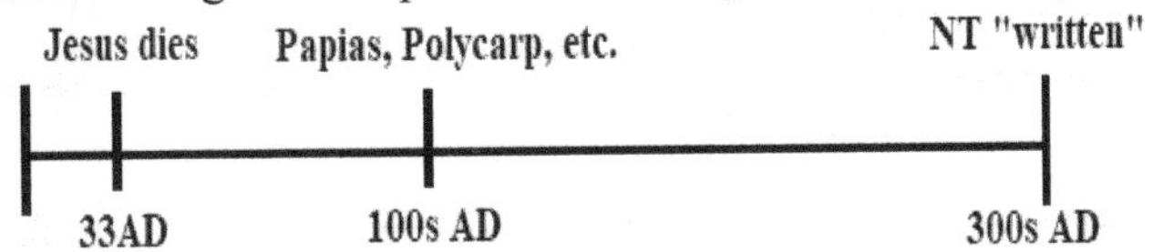

If the New Testament was not written until three or four hundred years after the life and death of Jesus as Internet "scholars" suggest, how could Polycarp, Papias, and Ignatius reference the New Testament?

Challenge 4

Skeptic: The teachings of Christianity developed over hundreds of years. Why trust a story that is nothing more than a legendary tale?
Christian: How does one convert to a belief system that does not yet exist? (There are multiple questions that could be asked in response)

Dating the New Testament earlier as opposed to later is important, however, it is not essential. There are other questions and issues that are important and relevant.

Moving past Herodotus and Hannibal, we answer our fourth challenge as it piggy backs on challenge three. Twitter and online comment sections are rife with arguments suggesting the Christianity's beliefs were established at the Council of Nicaea in 325 AD. Some students hold this position coming into Applied.

If it took hundreds of years for the New Testament to be written, and for the beliefs of Christianity to be established, then the faith students are basing their lives on is suspect. Demonstrating consistency between Christianity's origins and later developments assures students that their faith is rooted in history.

The credibility of the New Testament increases the earlier it was written. Likewise, if it can be shown that Christian doctrine existed earlier rather than later, the reliance we can give it increases, too. So, what about the about the origins of Christianity and its initial beliefs? When were they created?

An easy question with an even easier answer!

Earlier in this book, Paul was mentioned as a central figure in Acts and Christianity (Prior to 64 AD). Paul persecuted Christians before converting a few years after Jesus's death (33 AD). Here is the contention:

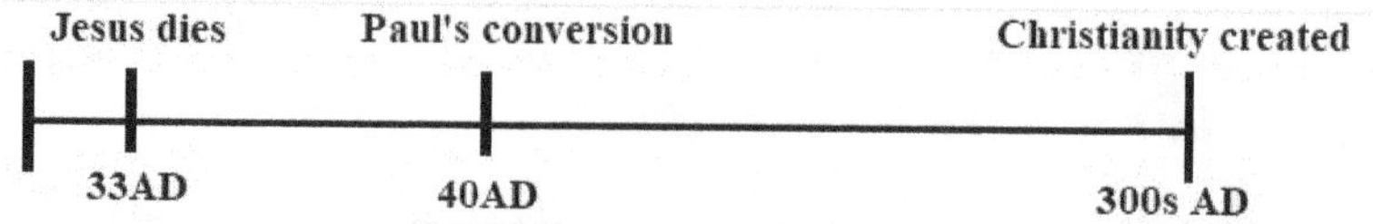

We are led to believe by some that Christianity's beliefs evolved over centuries or were not even created until the 4th century. Our timeline above shows that history disagrees. For Paul to convert to Christianity, Christianity had to first exist!

Paul's Conversion to Christianity before 40 AD proves Christianity existed well before the 4th century. Furthermore, Paul records the initial beliefs of Christianity extensively, and in many cases indicates that he received what he learned from the first Christians, or at least that he compared his beliefs with them, and they were the same.[103]

This simple exercise allows us to see that Christianity's early beliefs can be traced to within years, if not sooner, of the death and resurrection of Jesus; not hundreds of years or even decades later.

Brian Flemming accidentally supports this assertion in his anti-Christian video, *The God Who wasn't There.* Flemming spends his time regurgitating debunked arguments against Christianity but admits Paul's early conversion and responsibility in penning thirteen of the twenty-seven New Testament writings before his death, which was sometime in the middle of the 60s AD.

What Flemming should have done was make a case against the existence of Paul. Why? By admitting Paul existed and wrote a substantial amount of the New Testament, Flemming blunders by adding credibility to Christianity's origins, teachings, and practices.

Paul's writings include claims of Jesus's divinity, resurrection, and new practices and teachings of Christianity—all within years of Jesus's death. Flemming's swing and miss answers one of the most common concerns young men and women have regarding Christianity's origin.

On behalf of a grateful Christian Mr. Flemming, "Thank you!"

Assertions that the New Testament was written too long after the events and that Christian beliefs evolved over hundreds of years is not supported by the historical record. Christianity's origins were quick and humble, spreading from Jerusalem to Rome under threat of persecution.[104]

---

[103] 1 Corinthians 15

[104] Christianity did not spread by the sword. The oft cited crusades were in retaliation of Muslims capturing Jerusalem, a point ignored by politicians and liberal media outlets. Christianity was not in power until the 4th century. This is not justification for the crusades. Historically, this is the truth.

Reinforcing dates and ideas discussed in class, students are partnered up with my colleagues who sacrifice their free period and act as skeptics. Watching students interact with their teachers from other disciplines is both instructional and enjoyable.

Incoming teachers are provided prompts that students are invited to refute. In their response, students are required to draw timelines while verbally walking the antagonist through the answer. Students are provided not only knowledge, understanding, and application of content, but also training in how to use the information in conversational form if needed.

Chapter 9

Corrupt Christianity, Corrupt Scripture

Historical names and dates do not excite students very much.

Applied's first semester concludes with Chapter 9's content. Practical theology starts second semester off strong. Nonetheless, rather than disrupting *Applied Christianity's* flow, we will continue with our historical analysis. Here are more misguided assumptions brought into the classroom:

1. The Bible's content has changed over time.
2. Christianity selectively chose which books would make up the New Testament to control people.
3. The divinity of Jesus was created at the Council of Nicaea.
4. The Bible contradicts itself and therefore cannot be trusted.

Secular society seeks to undermine the New Testament by suggesting it lacks credibility. Dismissing the New Testament provides freedom to hold positions contrary to Gods Word, like abortion, homosexuality, fornication, drunkenness, etc. If the New Testament is God's trusted Word, then society, and Christians, would have to reconsider their positions.[105] One can understand why that would make many people very uncomfortable.

One of the most common preconceived notions brought into the classroom is that Christianity selectively, and with political bias, chose which books would be in the Bible. As the conspiracy goes, this process was completed under a shroud of secrecy at the Council of Nicaea in 325 AD.

Dan Brown's 2003 *The Da Vinci Code* is to be 'thanked' for making this assumption mainstream. His work is used as the day's anticipatory set as we read page two hundred thirty-one. [106]

Students are to identify Brown's direct assaults on the New Testament's foundation.

Three quotes become our focus:

1. "Man created it [the Bible] as a historical record of tumultuous times, and it has evolved *through countless translations, additions and revisions"* [Emphasis added]

---

[105] I am aware that some people just have questions and do not have a hostile approach to Christianity or the New Testament.

[106] Most of the students have not read the book, they are familiar with the idea because it is pasted all over the Internet. They are simply repeating what they have read unquestioningly.

2. "More than eighty gospels were considered for the New Testament, and yet only a relative few were chosen for inclusion-Matthew, Mark, Luke, and John among them."
3. "The fundamental irony of Christianity. The Bible, as we know it today was collated by the pagan Roman emperor Constantine the Great."

Readers of *The Da Vinci Code* felt vindicated, "I knew the church was lying to me all this time." Their dismissal was too hasty.

Challenge 1

Skeptic: The Bible's content changed over time.

Considering many students believe this false assertion, data and information which is new to them is presented in the form of a handout that I first expect them to decipher, discern and apply on their own. When they are done sorting through the material on their own, I step in and guide them through the information adding my own knowledge and expertise. Over the next two weeks we will analyze four different handouts. Handout one is taken from Carm.org:[107]

Author	Date Written	Earliest Copy	Approximate Time Span between original & copy	Number of Copies	Accuracy of Copies
Lucretius	died 55 or 53 B.C.		1100 yrs.	2	----
Pliny	A.D. 61-113	A.D. 850	750 yrs.	7	----
Plato	427-347 B.C.	A.D. 900	1200 yrs.	7	----
Demosthenes	4th Cent. B.C.	A.D. 1100	800 yrs.	8	----
Herodotus	480-425 B.C.	A.D. 900	1300 yrs.	8	----
Suetonius	A.D. 75-160	A.D. 950	800 yrs.	8	----
Thucydides	460-400 B.C.	A.D. 900	1300 yrs.	8	----
Euripides	480-406 B.C.	A.D. 1100	1300 yrs.	9	----
Aristophanes	450-385 B.C.	A.D. 900	1200	10	----
Caesar	100-44 B.C.	A.D. 900	1000	10	----

[107] https://carm.org/manuscript-evidence

Livy	59 BC- AD 17	—	???	20	—
Tacitus	circa A.D. 100	A.D. 1100	1000 yrs.	20	—
Aristotle	384-322 B.C.	A.D. 1100	1400	49	—
Sophocles	496-406 B.C.	A.D. 1000	1400 yrs.	193	—
Homer (Iliad)	900 B.C.	400 B.C.	500 yrs.	643	95%
New Testament	1st Cent. A.D. (A.D. 50-100)	2nd Cent. A.D. (c. A.D. 130 f.)	less than 100 years	5600	99.5%

Including Tacitus, Livy, and Herodotus, a few names look familiar. Column six is one of the more surprising pieces of data and information as it shows there being over 5,600 catalogued Greek manuscripts of the New Testament. This number includes fragments as small as an index card and as big as a full copy of the New Testament.[108] Other copies consist of full pages, complete chapters, or books of the New Testament.

Scholars, much smarter than I, compare these manuscripts to check for consistency. Their research has shown that the level of consistency within these manuscripts, from a variety of geographical locations, is 99.5%. While impressed with a 99.5% consistency rate, students inquire as to the other .5%.

Handout two, a page from Nestle-Aland's Greek New Testament, is presented as data and information to help the student answer that question. Most stare at the Greek, clueless as to what they are viewing. Patting themselves on the back, others draw upon their math and physics classes to identify the language as Greek.[109] Despite being able to pinpoint the language, students are oblivious to the handout's purpose. Enter, their intrepid instructor.

Drawing upon my limited knowledge and experience of Greek, I impress students by reading the first few verses from John 1:1-3 before drawing their attention to the variants on the bottom. The .5% represents small and some large variations from one manuscript to the next. Often a textual difference is a matter of punctuation, word order, or spelling.

---

[108] The Codex Sinaiticus is dated to about 350 AD.

[109] Others identify the photocopied document as Greek because they remember seeing the Greek letters from fraternities or sororities.

An example of a larger discrepancy is Mark 16:9-16 which Christian publishers almost always acknowledge as being ambiguously sourced in their editions. Certain manuscripts do not contain Mark 16:9-16, prompting editors interested in transparency to direct their readers to explanatory footnotes.

New Testament manuscript accuracy becomes more impressive when remembering scholars have access to over 20,000 pieces and copies of the New Testament in languages other than its original language, Greek. Manuscript experts have over 25,000 small,[110] medium and large[111] manuscripts to compare the New Testament against itself to verify consistency of transmission. If the New Testament changed drastically over 2,000 years, it would be of great concern... but it would also be quite obvious. Analysis however demonstrates the New Testament has survived for centuries, overwhelmingly intact.

Students are pleased to discover that the third document I have for them is at least in English. Depending on the year, students are furnished photocopied work from either Papias, Polycarp, or Ignatius. These authors wrote after the New Testament period but well before 325 AD. Referred to as ante-Nicene church fathers because they antecede the council of Nicaea in 325 AD, these church fathers are invaluable resources.

Ante-Nicene church authors constantly refer to and quote the New Testament, providing another available option to verify transmission of the New Testament. Ante-Nicene writings which quote, and reference Scripture, allow another opportunity to determine whether Scripture and the teachings of Christianity changed over time. If the church fathers that immediately came after the apostles egregiously changed New Testament content, doubt would be justified.

However, they quote extensively from the books in our New Testament, and those quotations are overwhelmingly consistent with what we have recorded in the New testament. Two-thousand years and counting, our Christian Scriptures and beliefs remain consistent.

This is a point recognized by manuscript scholar Bart Ehrman (non-believer), invoking his mentor, Bruce Metzger (who is a Christian), to illustrate:

> If he [Metzger] and I were put in a room and asked to hammer

[110] Rylands Library Papyrus P52 is one of the earliest and smallest manuscripts of John's Gospel, consisting of words from five verses from Chapter 18.

[111] The Chester Beatty Papyri collection is an extensive collection of New Testament manuscripts dated between 175 AD-250 AD.

> out a consensus statement on what the New Testament probably looked like, there would be very few points of disagreement-maybe *one or two dozen* out of many thousands. The position I argue for in *Misquoting Jesus* does not actually stand at odds with Prof. Metzger's position that the essential Christian beliefs are not affected by textual variants in the manuscript tradition of the New Testament.[112] [Emphasis added]

Available research demonstrates the New Testament has been saved from significant corruption. The most reasonable and honest conclusion is that the Christian Scriptures, along with Christianity's beliefs, have survived during two-thousand years of transmission.

What about the Old Testament? Answering that question are the Dead Sea Scrolls which are dated to 250BC-100 AD. The Dead Sea Scrolls are a collection of Old Testament writings found in the 1940s. Prior to finding the Dead Sea Scrolls, one of the most authoritative manuscripts of the Old Testament was the Masoretic Text of the 10th century.

Separated by more than 1,000 years, the scrolls and the Masoretic Text were compared. Lacking identical perfection, comparisons showed the Old Testament had also passed the consistency of transmission test. The Jewish Publication Society's Hebrew Old Testament introduction states, [113]

> Amazingly, manuscript differences are truly minor. More than 99.9 percent of the time, the masoretic Bible's witnesses give identical accounts. Rarely does the variation impact the meaning of a given verse.

Expectations and assumptions are shattered once looking at the evidence. Disappointed, the skeptic moves onto yet another challenge to undermine Scripture.

Challenge Two and Three

Skeptic: Christianity selectively chose which books would make up the New Testament to control people, and,
Skeptic The divinity of Jesus was created at the Council of Nicaea.

---

[112] This quote is from bonus material provided at the end of his book, *Misquoting Jesus.* To be fair to Ehrman, he makes the case that there are some passages which influence how one interprets a specific book of Scripture. These concerns are responded to in detail by Timothy Paul Jones's, *Misquoting Truth: A guide to the Fallacies of Bart Ehrman's Misquoting Jesus.*

[113] Jewish Publication Society, 2000

Using the right online hashtag will result in a plethora of absurd criticisms of the church such as, "Didn't you know, Mathew, Mark, Luke, and John made it to the final four out a battle of more than eighty possible Gospels?" or, "Seeking to hide the truth about Jesus and Christianity, the Council of Nicaea burned rejected gospels." Those who have not done the appropriate research are convinced.

Challenges two and three also collapse under basic mathematical reasoning.[114] As in challenge one, eager students are provided handouts that lack direct answers.[115] Up for discussion today is Josephus, Tatian, Marcion, the Muratorian fragment, and an extensive chart from Ntcanon.org. [116]

"Here is your problem," I say, "find the solution. Good luck." Expectations are high in Applied. Colleges expect pupils to know how to read and write. Professors are not in the business of holding students' hands, nor am I.

Josephus will take a momentary backseat to Tatian and Marcion as we address the question, "Did Council of Nicaea Christians choose Matthew, Mark, Luke, and John to be "the four" Gospels of the New Testament?" No.

First, evidence is lacking to support the assertion the Council of Nicaea had anything to do with selecting New Testament writings. It is a fun accusation to make, but it is with little basis. What the evidence does show is that the council was a gathering of bishops that hashed out wording to explain the already existing belief in the Trinity.[117] Our Nicene Creed was the fruit of their conversation.

Second, historical common sense demonstrates that the four Gospels had already rose to prominence within the church. With Marcion on deck, handout one contains an image of Tatian's Diatessaron with a brief explanation of his work. Tatian was a second century convert to Christianity. His Diatessaron sought to harmonize the *four* already accepted Gospels into one account. Which Gospels did he choose to harmonize? Matthew, Mark, Luke, and John.

His harmonization is dated to the last quarter of the second century. For visual effect, see the following timeline.

---

[114] 99.5% consistency between 5,600 Greek manuscripts from different time periods and geographic locations makes a strong case for transmission of Scripture.

[115] Reading historical documents during your second semester of your senior year with Easter Break around the corner is not a thrilling exercise.

[116] http://ntcanon.org/table.shtml

[117] Christians are aware that the word, "Trinity" is not found within Scripture. The concept is found both in the Old and New Testament. Plenty of books address this concern.

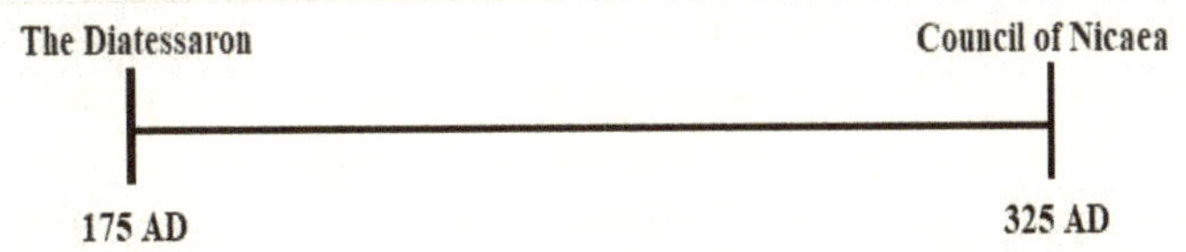

Remember what the challenge was? Here it is again: The Council of Nicaea, held in 325 AD, was responsible for declaring Matthew, Mark, Luke, and John the authoritative Gospels of the Christian church.

Glance at the timeline again and note *when* Tatian harmonized the four Gospels. I was never a strong mathematician, but I can say with confidence that 175 AD predates 325 AD. Already in 175 AD the four Gospels of Matthew, Mark, Luke, and John had risen to prominence.

Marcion, adds additional insight. Marcion did not agree with 1st century Christian theology. He felt so strongly about it that in the second century, Marcion decided to make his own list of authoritative books of the Bible. Furthermore, he suggested that the Old Testament was incompatible with the New Testament. Marcion was excommunicated in 144 AD. The purpose of invoking Marcion is not to discuss the things they were disputing, but to note that by telling us what he disagreed with, he illuminated for us which books the Christian Church were accepting as authoritative.

Quoting *The Da Vinci Code*, "The fundamental irony of Christianity. The Bible, as we know it today was collated by the pagan Roman emperor Constantine the Great."

Follow this line of reasoning: For Marcion to accomplish his goal of creating his own list, he had to first disagree with an *already existing list of accepted books* of the New Testament. Marcion's excommunication for challenging the existing authoritative books of Scripture was in 144 AD, preceding the Council of Nicaea by 181 years.

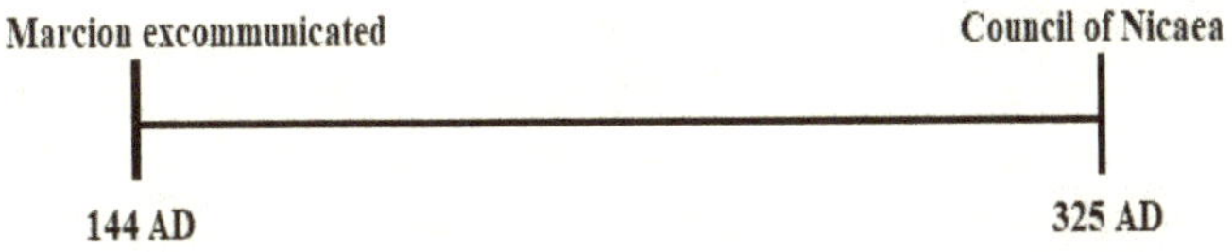

Common sense demonstrates there was an existing list of authoritative works predating 325 AD. Are we to believe that someone who was not even born (Constantine) until 227 AD manipulated a list of New Testament books in 144 AD?

Apart from Tatian and Marcion, the Muratorian Fragment contains a list of accepted New Testament books which corresponds to 21st century Bibles. A copy of the fragment in our possession is dated to the 7th century, but textual clues within the fragment point to an original composition of 170 AD. Here again, we have a list of New Testament books predating the Council of Nicaea and Constantine's existence.

Part of our assessment for this unit includes student's using cell phones to find tweets or memes that promote Dan Brown's lie and then responding to them.

The truth is, right from the earliest days, certain writings were viewed as more authoritative than others, and thus, received more attention and prominence within the first century Christian community. No veil of secrecy was needed.

What made these writings authoritative and rise to the top? We know many of the reasons. For example, certain writings were written either by the apostles themselves, or someone directly connected to the apostle. This is referred to as apostolic authority.

Placing the nail in the proverbial coffin, students are asked to recall one or two Ante-Nicene fathers from previous lessons. Within their writings are hundreds of references to New Testament writings. Skeptics believe the Council of Nicaea arbitrarily selected books of the Bible and even wrote the New Testament.

Yet, writings from the 1st, 2nd, and 3rd centuries contain New Testament quotations and references, and reference the list of books considered central to Christianity. This demonstrates conclusively that the books were written and chosen well before 325 AD.

Skeptics focus much of their attention on the New Testament. Occasionally, students wonder if Constantine had anything to do with the list of the Old Testament books. Exhibit 5,427:[118]

> For we have not an innumerable multitude of books among us, disagreeing from, and contradicting one another: [as the Greeks have:] but only twenty-two books: which contain the records of all the past times: which are justly believed to be divine. And of them five belong to Moses: which contain his laws, and the traditions of the origin of mankind, till his death. This interval of time was little short of three thousand years. But as to the time from the death of Moses, till the reign of Artaxerxes, King of Persia, who reigned after Xerxes, the

---

[118] Sarcasm reflecting the fact that the amount of evidence against the claim of Constantine's influence is overwhelming.

> Prophets, who were after Moses, wrote down what was done in their times, in thirteen books. The remaining four books contain hymns to God; and precepts for the conduct of human life.

Josephus, a Jew, wrote those words in his defense of Judaism against challenger, Apion. *Against Apion* was written after Josephus's first work, *The Antiquities* from 93 AD. Josephus's presentation of Old Testament authoritative works precedes Constantine and the Council of Nicaea by a *slim* margin of about 225 years.[119]

Presenting this information in mathematical form helps us understand both the challenge and the Christian response. Coupling historical common sense with basic addition and subtraction easily refutes the challenges listed above.

Next time a friend alleges the New Testament was written at the Council of Nicaea or the church chose the books of the Bible in 325 AD, draw a timeline using the information on the previous pages while explaining the truth.

Challenge Four:

Skeptic: The Bible Contradicts Itself.

Claiming that the Scriptures contradict is one of the most common challenges used by Skeptics.

Answering a question with a question, "Where do the Scriptures contradict?" Most people fail at having specific examples available as they are regurgitating lazy attacks that lack substance.[120] Asking a challenger for specifics puts them on the spot and places the Christian in a position of advantage. Gaining the upper hand is not intended to prepare for an attack against the accuser. Maintaining the high ground in the conversation allows us to dictate the direction of the conversation while educating the questionnaire. Most alleged Biblical contradictions can be dismissed with a little research.

Explaining the alleged contradictions becomes a necessity as some dismiss Scripture as God's Word if it contradicts. Students are quick to mention that differing perspectives do not equate to a contradiction. Matthew, Mark, Luke, and John have different perspectives which explain the same events. Many alleged contradictions can be dismissed

---

[119] More sarcasm.

[120] Circulating on the web years ago was a large poster of hundreds of alleged contradictions. Unfortunately, people posted the image believing they had triumphantly struck a blow to Christianity. Too bad they did not care enough to analyze the alleged contradictions or the source of the poster, a hostile atheist.

when examining the context of passages. Friday memory quizzes contain a favorite class tongue twister: a text without a context is a pretext for a proof text.[121]

What does "a text without a context is a pretext for a proof text" mean? When taking a verse out of context, it appears you may have proved a specific point. Proof texting is a common fallacy in today's world, especially in theology and politics.[122] Relationships are ruined because a boyfriend or girlfriend took a situation or words out of context.

Matthew 7:1 is a common verse taken out of context. Open your social media accounts and many shouting examples can be found "The Bible says you can't judge me. See, I proved it with Matthew 7:1." Seniors are provided a healthy list of principles to assist in dismissing alleged contradictions. Consider:

1. The verses immediately surrounding the text in question

How do the surrounding verses help understand the verses? In politics it would be smart to hear the President's words in their proper context before jumping to conclusions. It is no different biblically. How do verses 2-6 assist the reader in understanding Matthew 7:1?

2. The chapter it is found within

Does reading the rest of the chapter help in understanding that one verse? When accusing Jesus of wanting to kill His enemies, skeptics miss the part this part of the text is Jesus is telling a parable, that is, a story. There are thirty verses attached to Luke 19:27, but skeptics focus on just one.

3.The surrounding chapters

Our Matthew 7 example is a good one that illustrates the need to look not only at the surrounding verses, but also the surrounding chapters. What is the context of Matthew 7? Jesus's "Sermon on the Mount," importantly, also includes Chapters 5 and 6.

Matthew 7 is not to be isolated from, but included in, preceding Chapters. Jesus is challenging the hearts of individuals. Self-

---

[121] Biblical scholar Dr. Donald A. Carson attributes this quote to his father.

[122] Yes, even politics. Taking statements and viewpoints out of context is not something that happens only in religious debates.

righteous, hypocritical individuals should stop pointing their finger at others while ignoring themselves. When giving to the needy, do so with proper motives and not with blaring trumpets.[123] You do not have to literally pray in a closed room, but your intentions when you pray are to be pure. Your motives matter is the point, and this point is in view in Matthew 7:1-6, too.

4. The "book" that the verse(s) are found within

Looking at the context requires us to continue to expand our view beyond whatever the specific verse in front of us happens to be. In fact, these principles are not limited to resolving so-called Bible contradictions. Interpreting any verse requires us to explore the context in which it was written.

In that spirit, it should almost go without saying that we should be looking at the entire 'book' of the Bible in which the passage appears. Each author of the books of the Bible had their own particular reasons for why they wrote the book in the first place. (This is true for any piece of literature, by the way.) These reasons may shed light on how we interpret whatever the passage happens to be that we are looking at.

In the case of Matthew's Gospel, Matthew is focused on showing Jews that Jesus is the Messiah foretold in the Old Testament and that merely being God's chosen people was not going to be enough to save them. In the "Sermon on the Mount," Jesus was confronting the attitude that obeying the law to the letter was sufficient to make one 'right' with God. Jesus was arguing that the spirit of the law also had to be obeyed, that is, one's motives were also something that God judged. On that metric, even the most law-abiding Jew could not hope to be considered 'right' with God when it came to their eternal fate.

Can you see how that the *purpose* in writing can color everything written? Such is the case for each Biblical writer, and, as mentioned above, happens to be true for any writer, in all times, and in all places.

---

[123] Matthew 6:1-4

5. The Testament it is within

Is the writing pointing towards the Messiah or a reflection of the fulfillment of the Messiah? Are tattoos Biblical or are they not? Understanding the context of Leviticus in relation to Hebrews and the rest of the New Testament answers this question. Parents cannot shove Leviticus 19:28 in their child's faces because their children will in turn gently place Leviticus 19:27 and 19:19c back in theirs.

6. The larger Scriptural point of view

We also need to contemplate Matthew's *audience*. We can, and should, ask, "What is the message he wants to share with his readers?" Equally important is the question, "Just who are his readers, anyway?"

How does Matthew's Gospel relate to the Gospel of Christ? Matthew's Gospel contains the most references to the prophecies of Christ, which makes sense if Matthew is writing to Jews who are looking for a Messiah. Gentiles were not his primary audience. This realization influences how we interpret the Book of Matthew.

A key principle of Biblical interpretation is interpreting Scripture with Scripture. Here is the problem with pulling verses out of their context.

If you look at Matthew 7:1 and argue that the Bible says you cannot judge people, what do you do with John 7:24 which says, "Stop judging by mere appearances, but instead judge correctly?" This is a classic example of a proof text. "You can't judge me," people incorrectly scream. According to John 7:24, I can. Does the Bible contradict? Or, are we just taking verses out of context to prove a point?

Context matters. Jesus is not making a blanket statement against judging. Jesus challenges His listeners' self-righteous attitudes, a point made throughout the Sermon on the Mount. This view is supported by interpreting Scripture with Scripture.

1 Corinthians 5 directly encourages the Christian community to judge brothers and sisters within the church. Most Christians are oblivious to this passage and many others that encourage "judging" others. What we are judging is of emphasis. Paul makes it clear we are judging the actions of the Christian and holding the actions not up to human standards (self-righteousness), but to God's Word and His holiness.

7. The Language/culture context

Jesus calls the Jewish leaders, "whitewashed tombs." Understanding the culture of those being written about helps a ton. Stepping on a grave would make a Jew unclean. To prevent walking on the grave at night, they would "whitewash" the tombs to make them visible at night. On the outside they looked nice but on the inside was a dead, rotting body. This is an allusion that would have made sense to Jewish readers, but those from a different time and place would need to dig deeper in order to understand it.

How many alleged 'contradictions' are actually the conclusions made by people who are non-first century Jews who fail to appreciate the original language and culture of the writers of the New Testament? This is a question one cannot answer without taking the time and making the effort to understand the background the Scriptures were written against.

8. The Type of Literature

What type of literature are we reading? Psalms are songs and praises to God. If we take Psalms literally and out of context we come to many odd conclusions. Does God literally knit us together in our mother's womb with looms and needles? Proverbs is loaded with wise sayings that when taken out of context could be confusing, but this is what the skeptic does though. They take verses out of context and juxtapose different styles of literature and claim contradiction. We should be concerned whether the literature is poetry, songs of praise, statements of wisdom, narratives about someone's life, or Gospel proclamations.

9. The author.

James, for example, was the leader of the church in Jerusalem. Jews were pious and devoted to living holy (as Jesus pointed out, their pious living amount to self-righteousness). Reading James 2 in this context makes sense:

> What good is it, my brothers, and sisters, if someone claims to have faith but has no deeds? Can such faith save them? Suppose a brother or a sister is without clothes and daily food. If one of you says to them, "Go in peace; keep warm and well

fed," but does nothing about their physical needs, what good is it? In the same way, faith by itself, if it is not accompanied by action, is dead.[124]

10. The Law of Non-Contradiction

The Law of Non-Contradiction states that two mutually exclusive statements cannot both be true at the same time. Meaning, two statements that are not exclusive of one another could both be true at the same time.

For example, some people might object to how one passage of the Bible says that one person was present at an event where in another passage, two or more people are present. But does the first passage say that only one person is present? If the first passage has Jesus talking with just one person but does not preclude the possibility that there are more, then we don't have a contradiction. We have complementary perspectives, which, by the by, in the real world tends to be considered strong corroboration, as opposed to a problem.

Besides, I bet even in your own life you've shared an account like this: "I went to the store and I saw Jim. We had a good conversation!" Have you lied? Surely you saw more people at the store than Jim! If later on it is discovered there was a theft at the store and you were asked to recount what you saw while you were there, you would probably be asked to talk about all the people you saw there, not just Jim. Would your two accounts be 'contradictory'?

Of course not.

But that's just how skeptics tend to identify 'contradictions' in the Bible, and why we have called them 'alleged' and 'so-called' and 'supposed' contradictions.

Asking questions is a useful tool in the apologetic toolbox.

Challenger: The Bible contradicts.
Christian: Can you provide me with an example, please?"
Challenger: Not right now, but I know it does.
Christian: Here, get out your phone and open the Internet to Matthew 7:1. I'll show you a "contradiction."
Challenger: Wait, what? *You* are going to show me a contradiction?
Christian: No, I'm going to show you how to read Scripture and

---

[124] James 2:14-17

maneuver logically through these alleged contradictions. They do not necessarily contradict, rather, they are just being taken out of context.

Questioning the questioner allows the Christian to direct the conversation while educating the skeptic. While the Gospel authors and Epistles may appear to contradict, remembering that they were written by different people in different areas at different times, with different purposes and in different styles of literature is helpful in disposing of nearly all such accusations.

Chapter 10

Existence of Jesus

Breaking down historical apologetics into different sections and spreading the material throughout the school year helps both students and teacher. I know students are itching to discuss sex, drugs, and Rock 'N' Roll. I get just as excited to have these life influencing conversations. Flip ahead if you are impatient. Right now, we are going to keep plowing through our next historical topic, the existence of Jesus.

Few skeptics reject the existence of Jesus as a historical person. If Jesus did not exist, Christianity wouldn't exist, either.

Matthew and Luke both contain genealogies of Jesus. One of the first obstacles potential messiahs would have to overcome was whether they were from the correct lineage. American readers may not appreciate the importance of the genealogies, but it was one of the first boxes checked by Jews expecting the anointed one. This mere fact alone should point towards the existence of Jesus: Not a single Jew would have viewed Jesus as their messiah if He was not from the line of David, and obviously, if you do not exist at all, you cannot also be descended from David.

Secondly, manuscript evidence challenging the existence of Jesus is non-existent. On the other hand, Christian and non-Christian authors from the 1st and 2nd century do support His physical existence by referencing Him explicitly or alluding to His followers. Let's examine some of these.

Josephus

Flavius Josephus was a 1st century Jewish-Roman historian. His well-known and cited *The Antiquities* chronicles Israel's history.[125] Within *The Antiquities* are two direct references to Jesus.

I give the seniors a handout with the references reminding them that the purpose I have in showing them this material is simply to respond to the challenge, "Jesus never existed as a real person." Just what shape that response takes depends on their next steps. It is their task to work through the manuscript and use Josephus's words to prove the challenge answered.

Their first reading is one paragraph from *The Antiquities*. This paragraph is so famous it has been given its own name by scholars, the

---

[125] 93AD

Testimonium Flavianum. It is named such because it appears that *Flavius* is giving a *testimony* about Jesus, which, by definition, then, substantiates the claim that Jesus did exist as a person in history. After a few minutes of independent reading, students share insights with a partner. Hiding in the shadows, I listen for a partnership whose answer is correct. Josephus's *Testimonium Flavianum* is below:

> About this time there lived Jesus, a wise man, if indeed one ought to call him a man. For he was one who performed surprising deeds and was a teacher of such people as accept the truth gladly. He won over many Jews and many of the Greeks. He was the Christ. And when, upon the accusation of the principal men among us, Pilate had condemned him to a cross, those who had first come to love him did not cease. He appeared to them spending a third day restored to life, for the prophets of God had foretold these things and a thousand other marvels about him. And the tribe of the Christians, so called after him, has still to this day not disappeared.[126]

Josephus mentions Jesus was a wise man who existed. Case closed? If only it was that easy! Scholars are split on the authenticity of the passage. Look at the text yourself to see if you can spot three places where a non-converted Jew may give too much credence to Jesus. Why would a non-Christian make the case for Christianity if they were not also a believer? Scholars propose that later Christians managed to interpolate three sentences into Josephus's work to give the impression he was supporting Christ.

These alleged interpolations are:

1. If indeed one ought to call him a man
2. He was the Christ
3. He appeared to them spending a third day restored to life

It seems reasonable to suppose that had Josephus converted to Christianity he would have documented his conversion. These three statements seem out of place, and thus are considered interpolations.[127] Without these interpolations, scholars generally accept the *Testimonium Flavianum* as authentic. Here is the same text without the

---

[126] http://www.josephus.org/testimonium.htm

[127] A later 10th century copy of the Testimonium uses different language than the earlier 4th century manuscript evidence. This factors into scholarly conclusions that these statements are (or may be) interpolated.

alleged interpolations:

> About this time there lived Jesus, a wise man. For he was one who performed surprising deeds and was a teacher of such people as accept the truth gladly. He won over many Jews and many of the Greeks. And when, upon the accusation of the principal men among us, Pilate had condemned him to a cross, those who had first come to love him did not cease. And the tribe of the Christians, so called after him, has still to this day not disappeared

Even without the suspect interpolations, Josephus *still* attests to the existence of Jesus as a man who performed surprising deeds, called sorcery by the Jews, and was condemned to the cross by Pilate. Christianity was not a favorite friend of many Jews or Romans. Josephus could have ruined Christianity by declaring Jesus never existed and the story a fabrication of the highest degree. Instead, Josephus testifies to the existence of Jesus and His ability to win over 1st century Jews and Greeks.

Following the *Testimonium Flavianum*, in a separate passage, Josephus mentions, "James, the brother of Jesus, who was called the Christ." Skeptics may reject the prior passage but this one is a bit more difficult to dismiss. Obviously, you can't have a brother if you do not first exist! Yet, unlike with the *Testimonium Flavianum*, this passage does not contain anything controversial that can warrant suspicion, unless, of course, one is inclined to believe that Christians almost two thousand years ago were worried that thousands of years later, atheists would seriously doubt Jesus even existed. If one is inclined to believe that, one must at least give some credit to those Christians for their remarkable foresight!

Regardless of where one falls on the issue of the interpolations, at minimum, Josephus acknowledges Jesus's existence. Skeptics may concede this point, but they are not thrilled that Josephus was writing in 93 AD. They would contend that Josephus was not an eyewitness to Jesus and therefore cannot be a trusted source. It is because of such arguments that we recall again the writings of Herodotus, Livy, and Polybius. Much of antiquity is given to us not by original source material, but by copies found hundreds of years later or in quotations from authors removed from the original event. If our standard is only accepting eyewitness testimony from only original source material, most of what we consider to be 'history' would not exist.

Quoting from James Agresti's, *Rational Conclusions,*

> For instance, there are those who claim certain historical works cannot be relied upon because large gaps of time exist between when they were originally written and the oldest surviving copies. Yet, gaps of many centuries are typical when dealing with works that are 2,000 years old. In fact, the bulk of ancient Greek and Latin writings that exist today are known through copies that were made between the ninth and fifteenth centuries.[128]

Conversations of this magnitude are difficult if one summarily rejects everything.

Tacitus

The Annals, written by Roman historian Tacitus are less direct than Josephus's "there was a wise man named Jesus." However, we are not only trying to demonstrate the existence of Jesus by reading first century sources. Josephus, Tacitus, and Pliny present insight into first century Christianity without accused Christian bias. "What do we learn about Christianity?" is a reoccurring question when reading non-Christian sources. What do readers learn about Christianity when reading *The Annals* by Tacitus?

> Consequently, to get rid of the report, Nero fastened the guilt and inflicted the most exquisite tortures on a class hated for their abominations, called Christians by the populace. Christus, from whom the name had its origin, suffered the extreme penalty during the reign of Tiberius at the hands of one of our procurators, Pontius Pilatus, and a most mischievous superstition, thus checked for the moment, again broke out not only in Judæa, the first source of the evil, but even in Rome, where all things hideous and shameful from every part of the world find their centre and become popular. Accordingly, an arrest was first made of all who pleaded guilty; then, upon their information, an immense multitude was convicted, not so much of the crime of firing the city, as of hatred against mankind. Mockery of every sort was added to their deaths. Covered with the skins of beasts, they were torn by dogs and perished, or were nailed to crosses, or were doomed to the flames and burnt, to serve as a nightly illumination, when daylight had expired.

---

[128] James Agresti, *Rational Conclusions*, page 3

> Nero offered his gardens for the spectacle, and was exhibiting a show in the circus, while he mingled with the people in the dress of a charioteer or stood aloft on a car. Hence, even for criminals who deserved extreme and exemplary punishment, there arose a feeling of compassion; for it was not, as it seemed, for the public good, but to glut one man's cruelty, that they were being destroyed.[129]

Tacitus's insights into 1st century Christian are below:

1. Nero blamed Christians for the fire in Rome in 64 AD.
2. Christianity had spread to Rome
3. Christians were named such after Christus.
4. 'Christus' suffered extreme penalty by Pontius Pilate.
5. A problematic belief broke out in Rome and Jerusalem, was put into its place but broke out once again.
6. Christianity was thought evil.
7. Christians were arrested if pleading guilty to confessing the faith.
8. One charge was hatred against mankind.[130]
9. Guilty Christians were torn apart by dogs,
10. Nailed to crosses,
11. Burned and used as illumination devices.[131]

Regarding our initial question concerning Jesus's existence, Tacitus recognizes the existence of Christians, but also its founder, Christus. Skeptics grasping at straws argue Jesus was thought to only exist in a mythical realm. Tacitus shuts down that argument immediately when saying Christus, "suffered the extreme penalty during the reign of Tiberius at the hands of one of our procurators, Pontius Pilatus."

If it is difficult to have a brother if you do not exist, it is even more difficult to be executed by Pontius Pilate if you do not exist.[132] However, corroborating how Jesus died from a non-Christian perspective further enhances the strength of our case.

Another important insight offered by Tacitus is that the fire in Rome corresponds to when Paul was under house arrest in Rome as recorded in the New Testament.

---

[129] https://classicalwisdom.com/latin_books/the-annals-by-tacitus-xv/10/

[130] Christianity liberated men, women, and children. Christianity accepted the rich and the poor, the healthy and the lame, the master, and the slave. What hatred.

[131] And Christians are the hateful bunch…

[132] This is a historical problem for Muslims who believe Jesus never died on the cross. If Jesus died and rose, there is no need for a greater prophet named Mohammed.

True to form, skeptics attempt to discredit Tacitus by reminding Christian's that *The Annals* are dated to 115 AD and Tacitus was not Jesus's contemporary. If Tacitus is relying on testimony of others, he cannot be trusted, is their reasoning. This line of reasoning has been debunked too many times, including briefly in this very book, and in many others as well, but a refresher follows: Most of antiquity comes to us in copies of copies (hundreds of years later) or in quotations of others years removed (see Celsus below). Conveniently for the skeptic, these other histories are generally considered reliable, and Josephus and Tacitus, too, but not when speaking of Christianity. You do the math.

Pliny the Younger

Pliny's back and forth letters with Emperor Trajan has a solid page and a half worth of information regarding 1st and 2nd century Christianity. Three paragraphs in particular shed light on the question we are considering:

> Nor am I at all sure whether any distinction should be made between them on the grounds of age, or if young people and adults should be treated alike; whether a pardon ought to be granted to anyone retracting his beliefs, or if he has once professed Christianity...
>
> I have asked them in person if they are a Christian, and if they admit it, I repeat the question a second and third time, with a warning of the punishment awaiting them. If they persist, I order them to be led away for execution.
>
> They also declared that the sum total of their guilt or error amounted to no more than this: they had met regularly before dawn on a fixed day to chanted verses alternately amongst themselves in honour of christ as if to a god, and also to bind themselves by oath, not for any criminal purpose, but to abstain from theft, robbery, and adultery, to commit no breach of trust and not to deny a deposit when called upon to restore it.[133]

Pliny requests assistance from Trajan on how to interrogate Christians. Should he separate them based on age or treat them the same regardless? Pliny does not directly refer to Jesus's existence unless we allow that 'christ' is a reference to Jesus, but his insight on

---

[133] *Pliny the Younger*, Penguin Books 1968. Betty Radice's translation.

the beliefs and practices of Christians are instructive. Pliny records that as early as the 1st century and early 2nd century:

1. Christianity was spreading.
2. Confessing Christ resulted in an execution.
3. Christians met together before dawn on a fixed day,
4. Chanting verses alternatively amongst themselves in honor of Christ, who they,
5. Honored as if he were a god.
6. Christians bound themselves to a high level of morality.

Here in 2019, we have rejected chanting in honor of God, labelling it as archaic, repetitive, and rote worship. Early Christians relished the opportunity to worship God in such a manner.[134] Pliny's mentioning of Christians worshipping Jesus *as if to a god* is remarkable when we again remember that there are some who believe Jesus' divinity was not established until the Council of Nicaea in 325 AD. History once again challenges their conclusion as we have a non-Christian author showing 1st and 2nd century Christians elevating Christ as if He were a god.

Celsus

Celsus's late second century work, *The True Word,* criticized Christianity. Origen, an Ante-Nicene church father and Christian apologist quotes Celsus in his rebuttal, *Against Celsus*. If Christians were interested in suppressing criticism and hiding contradictory views, they failed. Origen repeats Celsus's accusations:

> Jesus was born in a certain Jewish village, of a poor woman of the country, who gained her subsistence by spinning, and who was turned out of doors by her husband, a carpenter by trade, because she was convicted of adultery; that after being driven away by her husband, and wandering about for a time, she disgracefully gave birth to Jesus, an illegitimate child.[135]

Celsus argues, without evidence, that Jesus was a bastard child. Although his argument was baseless, as with Josephus and Tacitus, Celsus admits the existence of Jesus, which is our concern for the moment. Thus, not only Romans sources, but Judaism itself

---

[134] One wonders if we will ever get back to the traditional roots of Christianity and the Gospel of Christ.

[135] *Against Celsus*, page 408, Hendrickson Publishers, 1995. Edited by Alexander Roberts, D.D. and James Donaldson, LL.D.

acknowledged Jesus's existence. Interestingly, while refusing to credit Jesus' works as divine, they did not deny that He performed the works, but rather attributed them to sorcery.

Finding manuscript evidence that challenges the existence of Jesus is, ironically, non-existent (pun intended).

Chapter 11

The 5th Argument for God's Existence

The Empty Tomb

Muslims need Jesus to fit their narrative that He survived the cross. Mohammed, to the Muslim, is a superior prophet to Jesus. If Jesus existed in the flesh and died in the flesh, Mohammed could still be greater than Jesus. If Jesus died in the flesh but also *rose* in the flesh, Jesus becomes greater than Mohammed. Jesus's superiority diminishes the status of the Koran and Mohammed. Indeed, both become irrelevant. More so, if Jesus did die and rise from the dead, it supports His claim He was the,

> Son of man, coming with the clouds of heaven. He approached the Ancient of Days and was led into his presence. He was given authority, glory and sovereign power; all nations and peoples of every language worshiped him. His dominion is an everlasting dominion that will not pass away, and his kingdom is one that will never be destroyed.[136]

Jesus's divinity places Him substantially higher and fundamentally superior than any anthropomorphic Greek or Roman gods. Buddhism and Hinduism take a backseat to the Great I Am. A risen Jesus indicates He is God of all Gods, King of Kings, Light of Light, the Alpha and the Omega, of which no comes to the Father but through Him.[137] No, not all religions are the same and no, we do not all worship the same God. Christ's resurrection emphatically answers the question, "What makes Christianity the right one?"

Our discussion on the resurrection of Jesus takes place at the end of the school year. Time permitting, Christ's resurrection is addressed via a mock trial. Students are assigned either the position for or against the resurrection of Christ. Research time is provided to ensure cases are strong and rooted in information. Each side calls expert witnesses and cross-examines opposing witnesses. Both sides believe the opposing side has the easier job, but preparation, knowledge, and application of information dictates which side will be victorious. Either you are prepared, or you are not. Freshmen, sophomores, and juniors from

---

136 Daniel 7:13-14
137 John 14:6

study halls are selected to act as jury members, with Magistrate Horvath presiding.

The trial has occurred no more than five times in almost twenty years of teaching. Every year more content and insights are added to the curriculum. Certain years offer more dialogue than others preventing adequate time for a trial. Make no mistakes about it, the stakes are high. Knowing that we may not get to the mock trial at the end of the year adds more pressure to present the resurrection in all content areas during the year.

If the New Testament was written by eyewitnesses who can be trusted, the case for the resurrection becomes strong.

If the New Testament has not changed, we can trust the content of the New Testament.

If the New Testament is supported by archaeology[138] and non-Biblical sources, accusing it of being fictional fails.[139]

If Christianity's origins were within days of the resurrection, and Paul converts to already established beliefs and practices of Christianity one can be sure that Christianity is not the result of legendary development. [140]

If Jesus *did* exist as a real historical figure and died, and Peter and the other apostles saw Him resurrected as they claim, then, *wow*.

These are only some of the major pointes of emphasis discussed in our current text and in Applied. When time runs out at the end of the year and we fail to convene our mock trial, classes are walked through the resurrection via lecture. Hundreds of books have been written on the topic with just as many points of arguments in support. The following pages will address some of the major points that lead us to a rather obvious conclusion:

> Something significant happened in the first century that literally changed the trajectory of history, forever. It was either

---

[138] Readers are directed to the Biblical Archaeological Society for a plethora of archaeological finds that support people, places, and events from within the New Testament. Because time is limited in Applied, the archaeological support of the Scriptures receives little attention in class. I can usually convey the amount of archaeological evidence during the year while we discuss other historical aspects of Christianity.

[139] Frank Turek points out that the Gospels have less than five statements of belief. The rest of their content are historical narratives of what Jesus said and what he did. You read that correctly: The Gospels are a historical narrative of the actions and words of Jesus, *not* what the disciples wanted Jesus to be. The reader is encouraged to read the Gospels with that fact in mind. The theological implications of the life of Jesus are found in the more accepted epistles.

[140] The Book of Acts explains in detail the development of the Christian church and its beliefs and practices. Pliny's insights corroborate the descriptions found in Acts. Acts 2:42-27, Acts 4:23-37, and Colossians 1 and 3 come to mind immediately.

the greatest lie every told, or Peter was telling the truth, "For we did not follow cleverly devised stories when we told you about the coming of our Lord Jesus Christ in power, but we were eyewitnesses of his majesty."[141]

The Resurrection

Paul's conversion happened within just years of the resurrection of Jesus. Textual clues from within the New Testament indicate Paul met up with the apostles shortly after his conversion to Christianity. The dating is crucial.

If Jesus dies in 33 AD and Paul converts only a few years after, the origins of the resurrection are not legendary, they are immediate. Upon meeting and learning from the Apostles, Paul later writes,

> For what I received I passed on to you as of first importance: that Christ died for our sins according to the Scriptures, that he was buried, that he was raised on the third day according to the Scriptures, and that he appeared to Cephas, and then to the Twelve. After that, he appeared to more than five hundred of the brothers and sisters at the same time, most of whom are still living, though some have fallen asleep. Then he appeared to James, then to all the apostles, and last of all he appeared to me also, as to one abnormally born.[142]

Within years of Jesus's death and resurrection, Christians are circulating a statement of belief declaring Jesus died, rose, and appeared to individuals and to groups of people. Peter claims he and other apostles were eyewitness of Jesus.

This is where the skeptics start grasping at straws.

A well debunked argument against the resurrection claims disciples and others, who were under mental and emotional stress, hallucinated a risen Jesus. While it is true that individuals under great stress can hallucinate, sharing the exact same hallucination among more than 500 individuals is beyond reason. Individuals would experience their own, unique, hallucinations. Suggesting Jesus's followers hallucinated an exact image of Jesus at the same time and location and were willing to die for their hallucination is beyond a stretch, it is irrational.[143]

Speaking of irrational, so are these claims:

---

[141] 2 Peter 1:16.

[142] 1 Corinthians 15:3-8

[143] Hallucinations do not last indefinitely. Sooner or later those claiming to have seen Jesus would have snapped out of their hallucination and back to reality, and disappointed.

1. Jesus moved the stone.
2. The disciples moved the stone.
3. The guards at the tomb let the disciples move the stone and take the body of Jesus.
4. Maybe the women just went to the wrong tomb
5. Maybe Jesus simply fainted, people thought He was dead, and then *voilà*!
6. Jesus was never put into the tomb because He was never crucified in the first place.
7. Is not it more likely the disciples and all of those who claim they saw Jesus were on drugs?
8. The story evolved over hundreds of years; therefore it cannot be true.
9. There are so many contradictions within the four gospels it is hard to know what happened.
10. The hundreds of eyewitnesses were victims of group think.

Plenty of books exhaustively respond to the shallowness of these arguments. Brief responses shared in class will be represented below:

1) Jesus moved the stone.

    a. Considering the ridiculous amount of physical trauma Jesus suffered before the cross, this is not plausible. Flogging was no joke. Some criminals died from the flogging alone. Add the additional physical damage experienced while on the cross, it becomes even more unreasonable to believe Jesus gained enough strength in three days to move the stone up the groove it would have fallen into. Remember, the stone was large enough that several people on the way to tend to Jesus' body were afraid that they could not move it, and they had not been flogged at all!

2) The disciples moved the stone.
3) The guards at the tomb let the disciples move the stone and take the body of Jesus.

    a. Are we to believe these scared followers of Christ who abandoned Jesus while He was being arrested and stood at a distance when He was executed, mustered up strength to take over trained (and armed) Roman guards? It is even more absurd to believe that the

Roman guards watched as the disciples moved the stone away and took Jesus. Strict penalties waited Roman guards who did not do their job: death.

4) Maybe the women went to the wrong tomb

   a. If the Romans were threatened by a new king overtaking their kingdom and the Jews wanted their blaspheming messiah executed, do we think the story of the resurrection would have flown? Here is our scenario: The women run to the tomb and finding it empty, run back telling the disciples, who also conveniently run to the wrong tomb, and the news spreads. Investigating the bogus claim, the Jews and Romans also go to the wrong tomb? They would have been the first to walk the women and disciples to the correct tomb to show the dead body of Jesus.

5) Maybe Jesus simply fainted, and people thought He was dead, and then viola.
6) Jesus was never put into the tomb because He was never crucified in the first place.

   a. Due to the mental, emotional, and physical stress Jesus experienced, He did not die on the cross but only fainted. Three days later, the gaping wound in His side is healed and His strength has returned. He pushes the stone up the groove and fights off the trained and armed Roman guards waiting for him on the other side. Sounds like we have a contender.[144] This line of reasoning betrays the fact Romans were top of the line executioners. Jesus was fortunate to be the one that slipped through the cracks (pun intended)? Josephus and Tacitus's words become more relevant:

Tacitus: "Christus, from whom the name had its origin, suffered the extreme penalty during the reign of Tiberius at the hands of one of our procurators, Pontius Pilatus."

Josephus: "And when, upon the accusation of the principal men among us, Pilate had condemned him [Jesus] to a cross."

---

[144] Sarcasm.

7) Is it not more likely the disciples, and all of those who claim they saw Jesus, were on drugs?

    a. There is not a shred of evidence to support this assertion. Josephus, Tacitus, Pliny, Celsus, or the Jews could have finished Christianity off early by letting the truth be known: Psychedelic drugs were consumed by more than 500 followers of Jesus. Yet, history is silent on any kind of claim of the sort.

8) The story evolved over hundreds of years, it cannot be true.
9) There are many contradictions within the four gospels which makes it untrustworthy.

    a. If the Gospels were 100% identical or different skeptics would be claiming conspiracy. While differing in specific details, the Gospels do not contradict. For example, one school year, a student broke their leg during practice. I asked witnesses to write a summary of practice including what they witnessed themselves. As one might expect, stories aligned but specific details were not identical. Everyone was correct in their conclusion even if their summaries were not perfectly aligned.

A common contradiction (alleged) raised to disqualify Gospel authenticity, challenges whether there were one or two angels at the resurrection of Jesus. In response, we ask a simple question: what prevents both accounts from being correct?

Let's use this specific example to rebut the whole category of objections.

In class, the Law of Non-Contradiction is applied to this scenario. The law states that two mutually exclusive statements both cannot be true at the same time. Let us apply the definition to Luke and Matthew's account of the resurrection.

Luke 24:1-4: On the first day of the week, very early in the morning, the women took the spices they had prepared and went to the tomb. They found the stone rolled away from the tomb, but when they entered, they did not find the body of the Lord Jesus. While they were wondering about this, suddenly two men in clothes that gleamed like lightning stood beside them.

Matthew 28:2-4: There was a violent earthquake, for an angel of the Lord came down from heaven and, going to the tomb, rolled back the stone and sat on it. His appearance was like lightning, and his clothes were white as snow. The guards were so afraid of him that they shook and became like dead men.

Luke writes two men in clothes stood beside the women. Matthew records an angel of the Lord came down from heaven. Logic states these two statements are not contradictory as they can both be true at the same time. If there were two angels at the tomb, there was obviously one.

If there was one angel (Matthew 28) there could also be two. Exclusive language would draw more concern, but that is not what we have, here.

"There was only one angel at the tomb" would be difficult to reconcile with, "There were exactly two angels at the tomb." The example is simplistic, but the implications are not. If they can both be true at the same time, and not exclusive of each other, then it is *not* a contradiction.

10) The hundreds of eyewitnesses were victims of group think.

    a. Would the disciples group think themselves to death with plenty of surrounding evidence available to keep their crazy thoughts in check? Scripture records that entire families converted to Christianity. Is it realistic to conclude that family members of the disciples were also delusional and victims of groupthink? To their deaths as well?

Regardless of the proposed theories, one fact remains: Jesus's tomb was empty. Every opportunity existed to redirect lost men and women to the correct tomb which would have been well known as it was owned by a member of the Sanhedrin.[145] Typical hallucination and drug theories fall flat on their face. Theories suggesting that scared disciples overtook trained Roman guards, or the guards let them take the body of Jesus, fall just as flat. Jesus's empty tomb and resurrected body was more than enough proof for hundreds of 1st century converts to

[145] Matthew 27:57-61

Christianity.[146]

When Christians are asked to prove the existence of God they could begin with the empty tomb. If the tomb is empty because Jesus rose from the dead, that is pretty strong evidence for God's existence, evidence worth dying for according to the disciples and thousands of others. And while it was impressive that Jesus had healed paralytics, the blind and deaf, more impressive was Jesus claiming to be God, healing others from the dead, and then, rising from the dead, Himself!

Jesus overcoming His *own* death, and proving it with an empty tomb, makes a strong case for a fifth argument for God's existence, with Jesus being God—which, is what Christians saw and believed then, and believe now.

Dying for your faith falls short of proving one's belief correct, though, a fact that prompts a need to make some clarifications on our part.

Seventh century Muslims followed Mohammed, who claimed to have experienced unverified revelations from god. Checking the veracity of Mohammed's claims was impossible, a truth that remains today. Jesus's ministry was opposite of Mohammed's in that His ministry was public. Jews, Greeks, and Romans had the ability and opportunity to see Jesus heal the lame and call out Jews. Thomas was able to touch and see the wounds of Christ. First century Christians were not blind followers as their faith in Christ was verified by His identity and public ministry.

Today, Muslim extremist kill themselves for what they believe to be true. Their experience is different than the 1st century Christians who were dying not only for what they believed to be true, but for what they saw to be true with their own eyes. It is incorrect to ask, "Would the disciples be willing to die for a lie?" Muslims die for a lie. Changing the question, "Would the disciples be willing to die for something they *knew* was a lie?" Muslims had and have no way to verify Mohammed's claims which is not the case for Christians today, and definitely not in the 1st century.

Concerned Christians (and/or skeptics) wonder if Christianity began as a fabricated story that went unchecked (not true) or was a part of a sinister plan by a small group of people to overthrow Rome.

> "Would the disciples be willing to die for something they knew was a lie that they themselves created?"

---

[146] 1 Corinthians 15:1-8

Many people will die for a lie believing it to be the truth. Who is willing to die for a lie that they *know* is a lie because *they* are responsible for its fabrication? Because that is essentially what is being alleged.

Furthermore, who is willing to die for a lie, *knowing* it is a lie because *they* created the fabrication *and* everyone around them would have *also* known it was a fabrication? More so, who in their right mind creates a lie, that everyone knows is a lie, dies for the lie, and convinces their family to die for the same known lie? Are we to believe these hoax creators let Nero crucify, or set them and their families on fire, or allowed themselves to be eaten by wild dogs, when they could have easily renounced their 'beliefs,' which they themselves knew to be a lie, since they were complicit in the lie's creation?

It does not pass the sniff test. Jews and Romans alike had access to the tomb. Knowledge of Jesus's existence would have been readily available. No single Jew converts to Christianity if Jesus was not an actual human, let one who did not fulfill Jewish prophecies. Nero's persecution of Christians was an excellent opportunity for the creators and followers of Christianity to deny their invented story.

And who converts to Christianity knowing that the entire story is a fabrication? Paul persecuted Christians before becoming one. Thomas doubted Jesus, so did James. Yet, both became staunch followers of Christ. James led the church in Jerusalem. Granted, James was the brother of Jesus and Thomas was a follower of Christ, but that fails to explain why other skeptical Jews, Romans, and Greeks converted to Christianity in the 1st century with a wealth of information available to verify or invalidate Christianity's origins.

Other arguments propose that select Jews created Christianity to challenge Roman rule. This does not make sense, either. Jews and Romans coexisted. Unless provoked, Jews had freedom to live their faith as they pleased. Does it make sense that a few Jews would create a false messiah who did not exist and therefore could not perform miracles and fulfill prophecies? Bad play. Forget the Romans who would laugh at their lame attempt. Fellow Jews would have zero tolerance for anyone within their ranks creating a fabricated messiah, especially one that supposedly was God incarnate.

Rome already controlled Jerusalem. Why would Paul, a Roman citizen who was overseeing and joining in persecuting Christians, convert to what he was persecuting, only to put himself into a position where he knew he risked death himself, and held true right on through until he was actually put to death? Why would he fabricate Christianity to compete with Roman authority that in important respects, he already possessed himself, as a Roman citizen?

Would you follow Jesus if you knew the resurrection was shown to be a fabrication? No way. Nor would the individuals in the 1st century who either were eyewitnesses or had direct access to eyewitnesses. Lives in the 1st century were changed forever as they confessed more than a resurrected Christ. They were confessing an end to the traditions and faith of Moses, Abraham, Isaac, and Jacob which had been established thousands of years earlier. For a fabricated lie?

Chapter 12

The Empty Tomb Changed Lives

Persistence in the faith saw 1st century Christians persecuted and executed. In Israel, death awaited those who confessed that they had abandoned thousands of years of rich Jewish history, faith, and tradition. To say the Jews were stubborn is an understatement. Old Testament writings are replete with examples of Jews either following God or wrestling with God.[147] Obstacles were an everyday occurrence.

Fighting for their lives and the promised land developed strong character and justifiable Jewish pride, which could get you killed or save your life. In *The Antiquities*, Josephus documents an intense moment between Jews and Romans in 27 AD:

> On which account the former procurators were wont to make their entry into the city with such ensigns as had not those ornaments. Pilate was the first who brought those images to Jerusalem, and set them up there. Which was done without the knowledge of the people; because it was done in the night time. But as soon as they knew it, they came in multitudes to Cesarea, and interceded with Pilate many days, that he would remove the images. And when he would not grant their requests, because this would tend to the injury of Cesar; while yet they persevered in their request; on the sixth day he ordered his soldiers to have their weapons privately; while he came and sat upon his judgment seat. Which seat was so prepared, in the open place of the city, that it concealed the army that lay ready to oppress them. And when the Jews petitioned him again, *he gave a signal to the soldiers to encompass them round*; and threatened that their punishment should be *no less than immediate death, unless they would leave off disturbing him, and go their ways home. But they threw themselves upon the ground, and laid their necks bare, and said they would take their death very willingly, rather than the wisdom of their laws should be transgressed.* Upon which Pilate was deeply affected with their firm resolution to keep their laws inviolable: and presently commanded the images to be carried back from Jerusalem to Cesarea.[148] [Emphasis added]

---

[147] Israel means, "to wrestle with God."

[148] http://penelope.uchicago.edu/josephus/ant-18.html

The Romans crossed a line by bringing in offensive images into Jerusalem. Pilate and the Jew's verbal negotiations failed, resulting in Pilate's preparation to slay the Jews. Josephus documents the Jews response to impending death, saying they "threw themselves upon the ground, and laid their necks bare, and said they would take their death willingly." Stubborn. Even to the point of death they were willing to defend their historical faith and promised land. Preemptive prompts set students up for a larger point.

> What would it take for the National Football League to give up outside sponsorship? What would it take for the NFL to move gameday from Sunday to Saturday?

An impossible thought. College football owns Saturday. The NFL would lose billions of dollars and so would colleges. If it happened, it would have to be one of the biggest, mind-blowing decisions, ever. Switch the roles if you must, what would it take for college football to move to Sunday?

For thousands of years (and to this day), the Jewish nation celebrated Passover. Then, one day, Jesus walks into town claiming to be God, while doing miracles, forgiving sins on His own authority, and gets himself executed. Then, mark this: weeks after His death, stubborn Jews, who only recently were willing to bare their necks to the Romans less their faith and traditions be offended, *cease* celebrating Passover and begin worshipping Jesus on Sunday, "as if to a god."

Two points of emphasis: First, asking a first century Jew to stop celebrating the Passover or worshipping on Sunday would have resulted in the same result as Pilate's threat: necks laid bare. Second, not only were the Jews willing to worship on Sunday, they were also willing to worship Jesus. Who in their right mind abandons Yahweh and worships Jesus, on Sunday?

In this context, resurrection conspiracy claims fail. What Jew would be willing to change their worship practices and focal point of worship for a fabricated messiah who never existed, performed miracles, or fulfilled Old Testament prophecies? And to the point of death? The empty tomb and a resurrected Lord are plausible explanations for such conversions. Mere words would not have convinced Jews to throw away their rich tradition and faith.

Abraham and Moses are giants in Judaism. Moses was given the laws of God to distribute to the Israelites. Sacrifices and offerings were to be conducted according to God's commands. God's moral, civil, and ceremonial laws were put into place to ensure pure worship and holy living. We ask again, is it plausible that our fabricated lie convinces Jews to give up divinely established laws of God provided through Moses?

Priests sacrificed animals on behalf of the Jewish people. Jewish converts to Christianity announced the Mosaic sacrifice no longer necessary. Christ had become the Great High Priest and The Sacrifice.

> Day after day every priest stands and performs his religious duties; again, and again he offers the same sacrifices, which can never take away sins. But when this priest had offered for all time one sacrifice for sins, he sat down at the right hand of God, and since that time he waits for his enemies to be made his footstool. For by one sacrifice he has made perfect forever those who are being made holy.[149]

What caused these Jews to shift from animal sacrifices to considering Christ's sacrifice adequate? Jews shifted from mandatory submission to the Mosaic law to professing that the Mosaic law null and void. Those who once considered the priesthood reserved, now viewed all Christians to be a royal priesthood.

> But you are a chosen people, a royal priesthood, a holy nation, God's special possession, that you may declare the praises of him who called you out of darkness into his wonderful light.[150]

Massive changes within Judaism required a massive and monumental catalyst for those changes; certainly not a lie! Families who had been practicing Judaism for centuries discarded their historic faith, embraced Christ, and changed the focus of their family's worship and practices for one reason: The Empty Tomb and Risen Christ.

These facts make another popular argument against Christianity seem odd, an argument first introduced to me by a student who had watched Peter Joseph's Internet video, "Zeitgeist." The video is largely a conspiracy video that begins with an attack on Christianity's origins, claiming Jesus nothing more than a copy-cat deity. Early Christians goes the argument, who created the lie of Christianity, stole attributes from Greek, Roman, and Egyptian gods that predated Jesus. Compelling theory, but without thought and research.

---

[149] Hebrews 10:11-14

[150] 1 Peter 2:9

Flemming's, *The God Who Wasn't There,* echoes Joseph's claim. Uneducated Christians would find this specific attack alarming.[151] Consider the prompt given to students:

Who am I?

1. Had twelve disciples
2. Born of a virgin
3. Performed miracles
4. Instituted a Lord's Supper
5. Was sacrificed for His people

According to conspiracies, you are the Roman god, Mithra.

Confirmed by their elementary schools only a few years ago, brief panic floods a few faces. Flemming does his best to make Christians and Christianity look uneducated, a bit ironic after viewing his video in its totality. Students are amused when Flemming shows a clip of atheist Richard Carrier accusing Christians of taking other people's word for truth and not verifying claims. As we watch Flemming's video we stop to critique his claims point by point. After destroying his arguments using common sense, students laugh at Carrier's assessment. It seems Flemming should have listened to Carrier's accusation.

Flemming's evidence used to support his assertion is non-existent or is an extraordinary reach. An image of Mithra's followers dressing up as zodiac signs apparently proves Christians copied Mithra.[152] Why not the opposite hypothesis, that Mithra copied from Judaism and the twelve tribes of Israel? Regardless, primary source material lacks supporting the creative assertion Christians copied from Mithra, Horus, or other ancient gods.

It is time to answer the skeptic with a question, again.

Skeptic: Mithra had twelve disciples and performed miracles just like Jesus. The Christians copied from the Romans.
Christian: What is your primary source for the alleged theft?
Skeptic: …

Historical manuscripts are just as silent as the skeptic's response.

[151] Having never been introduced to this argument in high school, college, or the seminary, I found it alarming at first. Truth be told, I never received any apologetics in twenty years of Christian education.

[152] Tektonics.org has been an invaluable resource for inquiring minds.

No one denies different gods preceded Jesus. We would expect gods to have similarities, like superheroes in Marvel comics. Early Christian apologists, including Paul, recognized this to be true. If your god cannot perform miracles, or lacks followers, it is not much of a god. Consequently, one can fairly expect that many 'god' claimants had various miracles associated with them.

Unfortunately for Flemming and Peter Joseph, educated skeptics have called into question their conclusions and research. Skeptic.com published *The Greatest Story Ever Garbled* by Tim Callahan.[153] Callahan calls into question the video's claims this way:

> Unfortunately, this material is liberally — and sloppily — mixed with material that is only partially true and much that is plainly and simply bogus. Joseph's main argument is that Jesus never existed and is in fact a mythical character based on earlier sun gods.

Asking for source material is a must for any Christian challenged with this argument. Callahan's biggest disappointment with Flemming and Joseph's are represented in his own words,

> Again, there is some truth to this, but Joseph mingles so much falsehood with whatever truths he reveals as to give ample ammunition to evangelical Christians who might want to shoot holes in his thesis.

I do not want to misrepresent Callahan. He certainly believes that Jesus is one of many gods floating around the mythical universe. But skeptics should be hesitant to use the copy-cat line of reasoning without primary source information to support their claim.

Having never heard the argument before I began to research the claim, I came up empty of any convincing material. One year when I was doing my due diligence preparing for a lesson being taught in my New Testament class, a portion of Acts caught my attention:

> Some of them asked, "What is this babbler trying to say?" Others remarked, "He seems to be advocating foreign gods." They said this because Paul was preaching the good news about Jesus and the resurrection. Then they took him and brought him to a meeting of the Areopagus, where they said to him, "May we know what this *new* teaching is that you are presenting? You are bringing some *strange ideas* to our ears, and we would like to

---

[153] https://www.skeptic.com/eskeptic/09-02-25/#feature

know what they mean." (All the Athenians and the foreigners who lived there spent their time doing nothing but talking about and listening to the latest ideas.)[154] [Emphasis added]

Luke's chronicling of Paul's work includes conversations with the Greeks and other foreigners who spent time doing "nothing but talking about and listening to the latest ideas." As Paul reasons and debates the Greeks, they are surprised by what he brings to the table: "May we know what this new teaching is that you are presenting?" These Athenians who had their ears in every conversation knew nothing of the Jesus Paul was speaking about. How come they do not challenge Paul, "We've heard about this guy before, his name was Mithra." or, "No, it's not Mithra, he's talking about Horus." or, "The Romans and Egyptians beat you to the punch. You do not bring us anything new." Instead, Jesus, the risen God is a new concept:

> The God who made the world and everything in it is the Lord of heaven and earth and does not live in temples built by human hands. And he is not served by human hands, as if he needed anything. Rather, he himself gives everyone life and breath and everything else. From one man he made all the nations, that they should inhabit the whole earth; and he marked out their appointed times in history and the boundaries of their lands. God did this so that they would seek him and perhaps reach out for him and find him, though he is not far from any one of us. 'For in him we live and move and have our being.' As some of your own poets have said, 'We are his offspring.[155]

Paul reasons the Athenian's Unknown God was an out of touch dead deity limited to the time and space of their temples. Zeus and Hermes have life and breath only in the minds of philosophers. [156] Christ is the living God who "gives everyone life and breath and everything else."

If this was old news, Jews, Greeks, and Romans would not have converted to Christianity, especially if it might mean their death. Jews would have sniffed out this fabrication straight away. "The Romans have already tried this one on us with Mithra. Now you use the same

[154] Acts 17:17-21

[155] Acts 17:24-29

[156] Acts 14:11-13, "When the crowd saw what Paul had done, they shouted in the Lycaonian language, "The gods have come down to us in human form." Barnabas they called Zeus, and Paul they called Hermes because he was the chief speaker. The priest of Zeus, whose temple was just outside the city, brought bulls and wreaths to the city gates because he and the crowd wanted to offer sacrifices to them."

divine claims but change his name? How dumb do you think we are, Paul?" And the Romans would have laughed, "Why are you using our gods and calling him Jesus? Fools."

Hundreds, if not thousands went to their deaths not for Mithra, Zeus, or Hermes, but for Jesus. Even more converted to Christianity, not because He lived in the basement of a temple or had cool statues erected with an obscure unknown name. Jesus was celebrated and worshipped because He broke through the sky, entered humanity, died, and was buried, leaving the tomb empty three days later.

Part IV

Influences

Chapter 13

Influence

Applied's strong points are the constant connections made from one unit to the next. Applied is worldview training and life training, all in one. Affirming God's existence and more, that *everything* in the world belongs to Him, means your girlfriend or boyfriend also belongs to Him—and not *you*. She (or he) is more than a piece of a flesh, she is a member of the priesthood of all believers, "God's special possession."[157]

Writing *Applied Christianity* has ignited emotions felt in Applied when covering certain topics. Capturing Applied's intensity in words has been a difficult task. Class can be rather mentally and emotionally intense, which is intentional. I want students pushed, pulled, and prodded, while meditating on life.

Students are surprised to find out I enjoy coming to school every day, sometimes asking, "Doesn't it get boring teaching the same thing over and over, every day?" Had I been asked that question the first few years of teaching, my answer would have been different. Since changing my perspective, Applied ceased being a chore, becoming an opportunity, instead. Responding to their question, "The content may be the same ever year, but students are new canvases who have never heard this content or its application. It's old to me but new to them."

Applied begins with individual exploration into one's beliefs. As the year progresses, individuals consider how their beliefs influence their friends, boyfriends and girlfriends, spouses, and society. Second semester's "Influence" unit starts with a caveat:

> The most important truth and life changing message I can share with you is Christ's Gospel. In all that we do and say, we start and stay at the cross where we see death being overcome and our salvation earned.

Watchman Nee's words are applicable to the caveat, "We think the Christian life as a 'changed life' but it is not that. What God offers us is an 'exchanged life,' a 'substituted life,' and Christ is our Substitute within."[158] I offer his words paraphrased in class, "Christianity is not about the changed life, but the exchanged life, His life for ours."

Keeping Christ as our focus during this unit is important because a lot of what we discuss is about how the individual lives the life entrusted

---

[157] 1 Peter 2:9

[158] Watchman Nee, *The Normal Christian Life*, page 119

to them by the Lord. Christianity is not about being a good person. It is about the Good Person and what He has done for us and as a result, what He does through us.

God has given us tools and resources to grow, His Word and sacrament being primary tools, our brains and the fellowship of believers being other tools. This unit is not about being the best 'you,' or about encouraging individuals to embrace a social gospel. Instead, Christians are to be aware of who and what they expose themselves to because the consequences are dire:

> So then, just as you received Christ Jesus as Lord, continue to live your lives in him, rooted and built up in him, strengthened in the faith as you were taught, and overflowing with thankfulness. See to it that no one takes you captive through hollow and deceptive philosophy, which depends on human tradition and the elemental spiritual forces of this world rather than on Christ.[159]

The influence unit focuses on three areas:

1. Influence of self
2. Influences of friends
3. Influence of college and living independently

Class periods still begin with opening songs or videos to encourage student introspection. Second semester's first three days start with three of my favorite videos.[160] Monday's video, "In the Words of Satan" by The Arrows, has become a class favorite igniting student reflection on the world and its diabolical influence.

In fact, I suggest you set *Applied Christianity* down and give it a listen right now, but then be sure to read Romans 1:21-32. Paul makes the case in Romans that God's people distorted His creation. Romans 1 points towards four areas of distortion which are well represented in The Arrows piece:

1. Thoughts
2. Actions
3. Desires
4. Worship

When we think of what it looks to love God with all our heart, soul, and mind, it may be wise to reflect on the focus of our thoughts, actions, desires, and worship. Are they directed towards the Creator of the

[159] Colossians 2:6-8

[160] In the Words of Satan; Propaganda's, "Be Present"; "This is Water" by David Foster Wallace.

universe? With the song in mind, students are asked a challenging question, "How have you been manipulated?" Students have a chance to respond to the question in one of their few homework assignments of the year.

Applied is a hands-on class. Students do most of their work in the classroom and hopefully spend more time reflecting outside of class. When seniors receive their two-page reflection paper as homework, they are a bit surprised at the out of class assignment. Every year I am humbled by their willingness to share personal insights in their reflections. Summarizing their responses in two words: True story.[161] Honest responders recognize society's influence on their lives. Moving forward the question becomes, now what?

Influence of Self

Step one is recognizing we are influenced by external sources. Step two is understanding how we have been influenced. Rev. David Maier and Rev. Bryan Salminen's 2011 article, *Change your Life: Think (...on These Things)* [162] is read in class. Three laws are introduced:

1. The Law of Cognition
2. The Law of Exposure
3. The Law of the Path of Least Resistance

Three prompts precede reading the Law of Cognition:

1. What do you think of yourself?
2. What do others think of them?
3. What behaviors manifest their beliefs?

Students write answers to these personal questions on the back of their handout. Combining with the Law of Cognition their answers are powerful. If we are what we think (The Law of Cognition), and I think myself to be trash, then I must be trash. Perhaps a student has a bad relationship with a verbally abusive parent who has convinced them they will never be good enough. If I am trash and not even worth my parent's praise, I might as well live in a way that reflects that conclusion. Our worldview conversations from first semester reappear:

> If God exists and is responsible for the creation of the world, then a human being is one that has been made in the image of God. If everything in the world belongs to God, then the broken

[161] One of my catch phrases in Applied depending on the year.
[162] Appendix 5 contains the full article, used with permission.

student belongs to God. Belonging to God means that His voice matters more than the parent's. You are a unique child of God, full of potential, washed in the blood of Christ. His blood has reconciled you to the Father. You are not what you think, but what Christ declares you: redeemed.

That conclusion is not possible if we have not first considered the implications and consequences of God's existence.

Spiritually and psychologically, "When our thoughts are healthy, determined, and sound, they will produce a good life. When the thoughts are diseased, unhealthy, destructive, and sinful, they can't bring forth a good life. You are what you think."[163]

I am not a fan of the phrase, "a/the good life." Considering that society and leaders within the church echo the sentiment of living your "best life now," it is no wonder young Christians are confused on Christianity's purpose, or reject it altogether.[164]

I prefer using "contentment" versus "good life," or even, "happy." Regardless of mountain top or trough experiences, one is still rooted in Christ in thought, word, worship, and action. All is "well-within"[165] when my foundation reminds me of Christ's redemptive and sanctifying work. Little else matters, so long as we are carrying out God's purpose.[166]

Our lifestyles are manifestations of our thoughts and worldviews. What we think about ourselves depends on what we expose ourselves to. Exposing our minds to unhealthy content undoubtedly has a negative influence on who we are, what we believe and the direction we head. Prompting students to consider this point, they are asked,

"What did you watch and listen to last night? What did you do?"

Hanging out with friends is great fellowship, unless their exposure leads (influences) you away from Christ. Listening to music is soothing, encouraging or motivating. Exposing your mind to music that encourages you to embrace sinful activities or harm yourself is unhealthy. Maybe what you were exposed to was out of your control when your parent(s) verbally humiliated you for not meeting their

---

[163] Rev. Bryan Salminen and Rev. David Maier, *Change your Life: Think (... on These Things)*

[164] Reducing Christianity's purpose to helping one's community and living your "best life" equates Christianity with any other religion or philosophical system that encourages it followers to help society while being a good person.

[165] When asked, "How are you doing?" I respond, "Well-within." Students recognize this as one my common catch phrases, but it reminds them that we are rooted in Christ and not our emotional responses or the days struggles.

[166] Love God, love people, share the Gospel. Matthew 22: 34-40 and Matthew 28:16-20

unrealistic standards. What are we to do then? Meditate on the word of God day and night, taking captive every thought and making it obedient to Christ.[167] Listening to depressing music is not the solution. Finding peace in the Risen Christ who has overcome the world is a better source of peace.

Christians spend most of their time and thought on non-Biblical concerns that have little to do with their purpose or vocation and more to do with themselves. Pressure, hurt, and stress build up and we lose "who we are" and "what our purpose is." Exposing our minds to Scripture and staying rooted in our Christian worldview will maintain our focus on Christ. Parents may carry absurd expectations,[168] but children live to first serve the King,[169] and only after that, their parents.[170]

Our reading leads to strong conversation and stronger application. Students find it difficult to argue with the line of reasoning presented in the article because it is true, and social sciences agree. Maier and Salminen's state the obvious,

> The events you attend, the materials that you read or don't read, the music that you listen to, the images you watch, the conversations that you hold, the daydreams that you entertain, these are shaping your mind, and eventually your character, and ultimately your destiny. Encouraging us to embrace teachings that are harmful to us or others shapes us in a direction we don't want to go.

What athlete, while pumping iron in the weight-room, listens to Titanic's soundtrack? We know music and television influences us. That is why we listen to music and watch what we watch. *Fast and Furious* was a popular movie series about attractive women, drugs, and fast cars. Theater parking lots were filled with adolescents revving their engines and taking one another off the line at the first red light. Ever watch a war movie and feel like taking on the world afterwards—until stubbing your toe? Confronted with actual pain, exposing yourself to real pain, and even death, doesn't seem quite as exciting.

Maier and Salminen's Law of Exposure is true: Whatever your mind is most exposed to, it will think about most. What enters your mind

[167] 2 Corinthians 10:5
[168] Ephesians 6:1-4
[169] Galatians 1:10
[170] This is not suggesting that children are not to obey their parents. I am responding to the unrealistic and misleading focus parents commonly provide their children.

repeatedly occupies your mind, shapes your thoughts, and ultimately expresses itself in what you do and who you become. Unfortunately, most of our time is spent exposing our minds to the pleasures of the world.

Discipline is required of anyone who wishes to start and stay at the cross with their thoughts and activities. Dwelling within the Scriptures and the perspective of the cross is no easy task as sinful individuals.[171]

Successful athletes and academics fight the Law of the Path of Least Resistance. Watching television and drinking pop is easier than committing an hour to the weight-room.[172] We were not created to be apathetic. Society has convinced us otherwise. Easier options include doing nothing, lying, cheating, or stealing. Quitting is easier than fighting. Spending time in Scripture is more difficult than watching the immorality of the Bachelor.

Training our minds to start at the cross requires effort. When our minds are focused on careers, academics, athletics, and relationships, we are not focused on Christ. It is easy to justify "I have more important issues to tend to than Scripture." Christianity is not something we do once a week, it is who we are in mind, body, and soul.[173]

Social media and the Internet make an appearance in the influence unit. Students are provided the day's prompt which inspires a few ignored eyerolls:

> "Why won't my children have cell phones?"

Sadly, most students know the danger of social media without changing their behaviors. Instagram and Snapchat allow men and women to compare themselves against social standards of beauty with devastating results. Behind a pseudonym and in the safety of your home you can slander, bully, or gossip unchecked.

Young men and women are being mentally and emotionally destroyed. Humans were created to foster deep fellowship with others. The Internet has connected humans in the virtual realm but has disconnected humans on a personal basis. Our natural desire to have oneness with others has been eclipsed by not enough likes or comments. With millions of users showing off their bodies via selfies, it is difficult to convince students to listen to one voice, the Lord's.

Our exposure rate to these dangers is hours per day. Asking seniors for advice on my own children's cell phone use is unanimous: Do not

---

[171] Romans 7:5-25

[172] Our friendship is questionable if you call it, "soda."

[173] 1 Thessalonians 5:23-24

let them have a phone. My decision was made long ago, but it is nice to see students coming to a similar conclusion on their own. Will they do the same for themselves and their children?

Former Facebook executive Chamath Palihapitiya had some not so kind words regarding social media.[174]

1. "Consumer internet business are about exploiting psychology. We want to psychologically figure out how to manipulate you, as fast as possible and then give you back that dopamine hit."
2. "I think we have created tools that are ripping apart the social fabric of how society work."
3. "I can control my decisions which is I don't use this stuff.[175] I can control my kid's decisions which is they're not allowed to use this stuff."

Palihapitiya later makes an intriguing comment that we feel more vacant after we post online. Our motives to post are to gain some level of attention (for whatever reason), but after we post we wait to see who responds or does not. Not receiving the desired results or our friends receiving better results leaves us more emotionally, mentally, and spiritually empty than before posting. "Susie liked my post, but John did not? Why? Is he mad at me?"

Considering what we expose our minds to is critical. Am I moving towards the cross or away from the cross? What influences are helping or hindering that process? Introspection 101 takes place in Room 101 and it is a no-holds barred internal fight. Knowing the influence media has on our spiritual well-being, students are given a challenge:

> Listen to only Christian music for 30 days. Compare your music to the teachings of Scripture. If the music you listen to contradicts what you allegedly believe, perhaps you should reconsider your selections.

Grading is absent from the challenge. It is their choice, not mine. How can a Christian justify music that glorifies sexual immorality while supposedly upholding the holiness of God?[176] No one should be surprised that most Christians are more secular in their beliefs and practices than what is described in Scripture. We expose our minds to

---

[174] Stanford Graduate School of Business forum: https://www.youtube.com/watch?time_continue=1283&v=PMotykw0SIk

[175] Keeping the book rated G. He uses a different word.

[176] Ephesians 4:17-32

secular media and agendas more than we do Scripture. One hour at church on Sunday is not enough to overcome the influence exposed to the other 167 hours the rest of the week.

Scriptural influence must play a more dominant role in the Christian's life. More so for young men and women heading to college, where secularism and subjectivism flourish.

Supporting the assertion that what you think matters and changes your behavior, students are introduced to *neuroplasticity*. Neuroplasticity is the idea that the brain can and does rewire itself. Constant belittling of yourself or others has a psychological effect, but also influences the physical development of the brain. Controlling our thoughts is not only important spiritually but also physically for the brain.

When considering neuroplasticity, the Law of Cognition and Law of Exposure take on new importance. High school is almost completed, and college is around the proverbial corner. Before you know it, you will be a washed up forty-something theology teacher with two kids and waiting to die.[177]

Life can be difficult. But how we deal with life does not have to be treacherous. Maintaining a proper perspective is key to survival. Our world's approach to life has shown to be one epic failure. Stressful and anxious lives do not have to be lived. Want to stop unnecessary drama? Stop arguing and caring about pointless issues. Stop complaining about the DUI, MIP, or LMNOP you received if you were drinking while driving. Care to avoid being in that situation and the related stress? Make different choices and set different priorities.

I get paid millions of dollars[178] to help students transition from high school to college-and beyond. It would be foolish of me to not prepare their minds and bodies as well. Meditating on the Word of God is an appropriate first step of action. Controlling your thoughts within your worldview is the second:

> Finally, brothers and sisters, whatever is true, whatever is noble, whatever is right, whatever is pure, whatever is lovely, whatever is admirable—if anything is excellent or praiseworthy—think about such things. Whatever you have learned or received or heard from me, or seen in me—put it into practice. And the God of peace will be with you.[179]

---

[177] A favorite catch phrase that most students finish before I make it halfway through.
[178] Another favorite catch phrase.
[179] Philippians 4:8-9

> The weapons we fight with are not the weapons of the world. On the contrary, they have divine power to demolish strongholds. We demolish arguments and every pretension that sets itself up against the knowledge of God, *and we take captive every thought to make it obedient to Christ.*[180] [Emphasis added]

Am I worthless? No. Am I ugly? No. What is my purpose? Look to Scriptures. The one who made you knows your purpose. Trust Him. Provided in class are four steps to taking captive every thought and making it obedient to Christ:[181]

1. Recognize
2. Question
3. Replace
4. Change your behavior

No one else controls your thoughts. It is *your* brain, not theirs.

Putting the four steps into action looks like this:

Perhaps the individual believes themselves to be worthless and not good enough. The challenge is to recognize the unhealthy thought. Awareness of your thoughts and their consequences matter. Recognize and question the thought. "Is it true that I'm worthless?" Replace the thought with a Christ-centered thought, "I have been made in the image of God. I've been bought with the literal blood of Christ. I am His."

If necessary, change your behavior. If you are looking in the mirror and reflecting on how pathetic you think you are, leave the room. Go for a run. Grab a book and start to read. Changing your behavior changes the thought process. Moments ago, you were thinking you were worthless, now you are thinking about how warm it is outside.

Better, go to your Lord in prayer, meditating on God's Word as opposed to your own words. His Word promises streams of living water, the world's words suck life out of us.

The four steps can be applied to any situation. Habit and discipline of thought influence your attitudes and behaviors. Knowing that what you are listening to and watching is leading you away from Christ is an important step towards spiritual growth. Take captive your thoughts and hold them against Scripture. Change and replace your thoughts and actions with Scripture as needed.

---

[180] 2 Corinthians 10:5

[181] Staying rooted in Christ and His Word is always priority one

Chapter 14

Influence of Friends

Incoming high school freshmen are oblivious to how new friendships are going to be developed, and how those friendships are going to influence their journey towards, or away, from the cross. Discussing meaningful friendships is an important conversation because seniors are about to become freshmen all over again. Bringing awareness to their new transition is our purpose.

College will challenge their mental, emotional, physical, and spiritual (MEPS) well-being. Maintaining a well-balanced MEPS is critical not only to their transition but also for life. MEPS has become a staple of Applied and is discussed in a variety of contexts.

Friends influence each other mentally, emotionally, physically, and spiritually—but it is not always for the better. Ninth-grade social dynamics are interesting to observe. Walking the halls and coaching athletes allows an observant teacher to witness the shaping of young men and women.

Walking into the classroom, seniors see red tape on the floor containing Scripture verses and MEPS:[182]

The tape symbolizes our moral and spiritual line.

Coming into 9th grade, freshmen may say to themselves, "When I get to high school, I'm never going have sex or drink alcohol." Screwtape and Wormwood have different ideas for their four years of high school. Screwtape directs Wormwood to encourage the patient to

[182] Memory verses are written on the tape to reinforce Scripture and the associated lessons.

choose poor friends. Read Screwtape's insights in the context of an incoming 9th grade student. The bullet point organization is mine:

1. And you seem to have made good use of all his social, sexual, and intellectual vanity. Tell me more. Did he commit himself deeply?
2. There is a subtle play of looks and tones and laughs by which a mortal can imply that he is of the same party as those to whom he is speaking. That is the kind of betrayal you should specially encourage, because the man does not fully realize it himself; and by the time he does you will have made withdrawal difficult.
3. No doubt he must very soon realize that his own faith is in direct opposition to the assumptions on which all the conversation of his new friends is based. I do not think that matters much provided that you can persuade him to postpone any open acknowledgment of the fact.
4. He will be silent when he ought to speak and laugh when he ought to be silent.
5. He will assume, at first only by his manner, but presently by his words, all sorts of cynical and skeptical attitudes which are not really his. But if you play him well, they may become his.
6. If he is a big enough fool you can get him to realize the character of the friends only while they are absent; their presence can be made to sweep away all criticism.
7. He can be made to take a positive pleasure in the perception that the two sides of his life are inconsistent. This is done by exploiting his vanity.

With a partner, seniors find examples of how each statement related to their 9th grade experience. I can usually be heard chuckling as they discuss the examples. It was only a few years ago that these same students were living Screwtape's tenth letter. "There is a subtle play of looks and tones and laughs by which a mortal can imply that he is of the same party," writes Lewis. Imagine the hallway full of freshmen, all laughing and joking around with each other without knowing one another. Biology class takes on a new perspective when students snicker at a new acquaintance's off-color comment. After school soccer practice now has the two acquaintances attached at the hip, warming up together and sharing disrespectful tones and looks towards their coach whose back is turned in opposite direction. Weeks later, the two are best friends. Two years later and having crossed the "red line," they sit before the assistant principal wondering how it all happened. Oblivious, the two morphed into a friendship their freshmen year. Wormwood receives a pat on the back from his proud uncle. Mission accomplished.

In the same class and on the same soccer team was a friend from elementary school who was kicked to the curb in high school. He should have spoken-up and tried to help his friend steer clear of the bad influence, but he remained silent. Why? He laughed at the jokes instead staying silent. Why? Who wants to call their friend out for bad behavior? People of all ages want to protect their "social, sexual, and intellectual vanity." In Applied we call this "social currency."

As our four years of high school progress, our social bank account increases. Deposits into the account are made by increasing our social status, sexual conquests, academic, and athletic success, etc. Some examples of increasing one's social status is vaping, bullying, disrespecting teachers and coaches, etc. Grade point average, ACT, SAT and LMNOP[183] scores deposit periodically into the bank- depending on who our friends are.

No one likes to be Mr. Horvath.[184] People want to be accepted. They want to fit in and be appreciated. Transitioning from middle school to high school finds youth in precarious situations not previously considered. Their lines exist but may start to blur as new friendships are established.

Social bank accounts are not necessarily bad. It all depends on what type of currency you deposit, and in which bank you deposit your funds. Even the "good student" with an amazing GPA can be found sharing their homework with their best friend. Your social status within the group may suffer if you maintain your integrity by denying your friend access. Try convincing a high school student to stand up to their friends from 1st grade, who are now drinking alcohol.

Many students increase their social bank account at the expense of other students. Bullying and gossip destroys relationships. So, too, does sexual promiscuity. And in the conversation with your friend about your sexual conquest, your sinful action and your glorification of your conquest makes a deposit into the Bank of Hades.[185]

Four years later and the seniors have been influenced by their

---

[183] Obviously not a real test. The joke earns a few laughs.

[184] I do my best to put the shame, guilty, stupidity, idiocy, etc. on myself as opposed to the students. Laugh at me while you consider if it relates to *you*.

[185] I've been told that some college students keep track of their conquests.

friends and a variety of shared experiences. Regardless if the influence was positive or negative, seniors were unwilling participants of social influence. They climbed the high school social, athletic, or academic ladder, but in a few short months, the graduating senior's bank accounts will be set back to zero.

Our conversation shifts from high school to college, which brings a whole new level of vulnerability. Safety nets no longer exist or are far removed. Mom, Dad, and their elementary school friends are hours away. Mr. Horvath is not in their back pocket. Chapel and Sunday worship will no longer be routine. Added to the removal of the safety nets is a new level of mental and emotional stress they have not yet experienced. New environment, new people, new vulnerabilities. Freeeeeeeeeeeeedom.[186]

Dorm room conversations are not like 9th grade biology class conversations. Friday's home basketball game is nothing compared to the fraternity party down the road. Asking the rhetorical question again, who wants to go to college and hide in their bedroom and not make friends? Alcohol is a known part of the college experience. Attempting to make friends while you make the transition into college adds more pressure to cross or erase your "line." Girls and boys are now young men and women. Pressure increases to find "the one." Without parents or teachers around, freedom is the name of the game.

Spiritual stakes are high. High school friends were friendships of convenience and circumstance.[187] Unless the friendships are mature and rooted in a strong foundation, most of them will not last past the first couple years of college, if not ending sooner.[188] This could be a blessing in disguise. Getting away from unhealthy influences allows the senior to grow into their own person in Christ. A new awareness of the social dynamic places the soon to be college freshmen in better positions for mental, emotional, physical, and spiritual health. How will they go about making new friends without compromising themselves or their line?

"When I go to college, I will never have sex, do drugs, or drink alcohol." Will they hold their line? Notebooks and Scripture are opened as students are provided five steps assisting in developing Christ-centered friendships in college.

---

[186] In class, I channel my inner Braveheart and let freeeeeeeeeeeeedom rip.

[187] Beloved teacher Robin Kearney shared this term with her students when she was teaching.

[188] Shout out to "The Core." A group of girls who took the challenge seriously and are still strong friends today.

1. Discern
2. Decide
3. Distance
4. Develop
5. Dependability Partner (aka: accountability partner)

High school freshmen are probably unaware of the definition of 'discern,' let alone possess the ability to discern between healthy or unhealthy friends. Conversation is primed by reading Matthew 7:15-23:

> Watch out for false prophets. They come to you in sheep's clothing, but inwardly they are ferocious wolves. By their fruit you will recognize them. Do people pick grapes from thornbushes, or figs from thistles? Likewise, every good tree bears good fruit, but a bad tree bears bad fruit. A good tree cannot bear bad fruit, and a bad tree cannot bear good fruit. Every tree that does not bear good fruit is cut down and thrown into the fire. Thus, by their fruit you will recognize them.

True, Jesus's warning is against false prophets, but the concept rings true for discerning between healthy or unhealthy friends. Does the individual bear good fruit or bad fruit? Are they loving others or only themselves?

Contrast the fruits of darkness found in Ephesians 4-5 with the fruits of the Spirit.

Uncontrollable anger	Justifiable and controlled anger
Thief	Working for one's possessions (hard worker)
Unwholesome talk	Speaking in psalms, hymns, and Scripture
Coarse joking	Appropriate humor
Slanderer	Builds others up
Hateful and bitter	Loving, kind, compassionate
Sexually immoral	Sexually pure actions and words
Obscene language and talk	Wholesome talk seasoned with grace
Greedy	Content in Christ
Drunkard	Sober
Lacking wisdom	Filled with the Light of Christ

Discerning which column is best is simple. Putting it into practice, however, will not be easy. It will be a choice and it will take discipline. Wise investments will reap positive spiritual dividends. Poor investments earning the opposite result may impact eternity.

Lifelong friends and future spouses may be found within the next few years of college. Who seniors choose to be and attract will influence how they raise their children.[189] Serving the world looks different than serving Christ. Seniors will have to decide whom they will serve,

> But if serving the LORD seems undesirable to you, then choose for yourselves this day whom you will serve, whether the gods your ancestors served beyond the Euphrates, or the gods of the Amorites, in whose land you are living. But as for me and my household, we will serve the LORD.[190]

During our conversation on friendships I am moving in and out of the red box taped on the floor. Graduating seniors are encouraged to place a footlong piece of tape on their college bed or dresser to remind them of their chosen line. "Decide," I say, "what your line is going to be and whether you will be willing to cross it for your new set of friends." Reminders of vulnerabilities are plentiful. Independent of their parents and high school, they will be holding their line alone.

Natural distance may preclude seniors from maintaining unhealthy influences from high school. College may require a more drastic measures such as a physical removal from new friends. Paul delivers bold instructions to the Corinthians on how to deal with those who are corrupting the church:

> I wrote to you in my letter not to associate with sexually immoral people— not at all meaning the people of this world who are immoral, or the greedy and swindlers, or idolaters. In that case you would have to leave this world. But now I am writing to you that you must not associate with anyone who claims to be a brother or sister but is sexually immoral or greedy, an idolater or slanderer, a drunkard or swindler. Do not even eat with such people.[191]

Harsh words, depending on your perspective.

---

[189] Worthy of reflection: What we choose to believe and how we manifest those beliefs will have a direct impact on our children and as default, their children. Your grandchildren.

[190] Joshua 24:14-15

[191] 1 Corinthians 5:9-11

Per the norm, a student will raise their hand asking a familiar question, "But aren't we supposed to not judge others?" Secularism within the church has created this myth. Post-modern America screams "You can't judge me," while judging those who are allegedly guilty of judging.

The oft misquoted text of Matthew 7:1 has already been addressed in Chapter 10. Context matters. Jesus is calling out self-righteous hypocrites. Christ is not banning "judging."

Readers of 1 Corinthians 5 end up confused because they have been misled and because they did not read the entire text. Paul directs the Corinthians to not associate with someone who calls themselves a "brother but is sexually immoral or greedy, an idolater or slanderer, a drunkard or swindler. Do not even eat with such people." It is not that you cannot associate with the people of the world. How else would the Gospel spread? Paul's warning is against maintaining fellowship with Christians who embrace darkness as opposed to the Light. Why? Bad company corrupts good character. Allowing a deliberate and unrepentant sinner in the community is dangerous. Expel the brother so they may recognize their sin and not harm the community by leading others in the same direction.

You cannot determine if the influence is healthy or not unless the actions are judged against Scripture and God's law. Quoting Paul,

> "What business is it of mine to judge those outside the church? *Are you not to judge those inside?* God will judge those outside. Expel the wicked person from among you."[192] [Emphasis added]

Judging the actions of those within the church protects the community but also the disobedient. Ignoring a disobedient sinner's situation places them in grave spiritual danger.

> Brothers and sisters, if someone is caught in a sin, you who live by the Spirit should restore that person gently. But watch yourselves, or you also may be tempted.[193]

Catching someone sinning should lead to gentle confrontation and if need be, a stern rebuke. Failure to care about sin is beyond problematic.[194] Judge the actions of those within the church to protect the sinner and fellowship of believers. Distancing and disassociating

---

[192] 1 Corinthians 15:12-13
[193] Galatians 6:1. Verses 2-6 are also informative.
[194] Hebrews 10:19-39

yourself from individuals who outright deny the faith they profess without repentance protects you from spiritual danger.

Students remain apprehensive about what to do with their friends who choose to live contrary to God's will. Do we kick them to the curb? Make ourselves available for assistance? Yes. Removing ourselves from poor influences is more a process than immediate removal (depending on the context).

An invite to the weekend party goes rejected. Instead of accepting the offer, ask the friend to join you in a more God-pleasing activity. If your friend rejects the offer, carry on with your weekend. Sooner or later, the offers will subside. Short and long term, this is the better option. Perhaps the friend agrees to join your more God-pleasing option, who knows? Directing and developing the friend towards the cross becomes a realistic opportunity for Christ-centered influence.[195]

Very few high school freshmen seek out mature, God-fearing friends. Now that we have considered the social, spiritual, and psychological dynamic of friendships and influence, graduates heading into college are without excuse. With lines drawn, beliefs determined, and foundations set, Christian discernment becomes natural. Do not go to the party. Do not associate with individuals who will direct you away from the cross. Choose differently. Develop and grow according to the Word and not the world.

Invest in those who can be depended on and will not leave you abandoned. Dependability partners can be our friends and mentors.[196] Whether at the top of the mountain or in the valley of a trough, dependability partners are those we can lean and depend on to keep us rooted in Christ. Your roommate may be a professing Christian, but they may abandon you for a frat party (or drag you along).

Identifying an older mentor who can walk with you through life is a viable and encouraged option. Relying on mentors requires humility, as older individuals carry wisdom outside a younger person's perspective. Humans were not meant to walk through life alone. Choose someone or a group of individuals who are dependable and will hold you accountable in your Christian walk. Regardless of who it is, if they are not leading you towards the cross, they are leading you away from Christ. Choose wisely.

Healthy friendships are critical to transitioning from high school to college. Depending on God's Word, weekly worship, and the

---

[195] Proverbs 27:17

[196] Accountability partner sounds better, but I wanted to keep 5 d's and not 4d's and one A. That seemed awkward. Discern, Decide, Distance, Develop and Accountability? No. Just, no.

fellowship of other believers is priority one.[197] Consider another option for growth: be dependable for others. Your roommate may be considering a frat party, but *your* influence may lead them in another direction. Dependability usually goes hand in hand with maturity. We may consider excusing incoming 9th graders for lacking mental, emotional, and spiritual maturity. Soon to be college freshmen who are provided resources, wisdom, and awareness are without excuse. Drawing and establishing spiritual boundaries in beliefs and friendships protects the believer from unhealthy influences. Know thyself. Know Him.

Placed inside the red tape which represented our moral and spiritual line, is now white tape which represents our mental, emotional, physical, and spiritual boundaries (MEPS). Students in class provide examples of establishing boundaries in college.

Physical boundaries would include not violating your roommates' space, communicating to your significant other that sex is not acceptable until marriage, maintaining a consistent sleep schedule, and eating healthy. Removing yourself from individuals who lead you away from Christ sets a spiritual boundary.

Our mental and emotional health impacts our physical health and vice versa. Staying rooted in Scripture establishes a spiritual boundary against false secular teachings opposed to Christ.

Maintaining mental and emotional boundaries are imperative. Saying "no" is not only a sexual line drawn in the sand. Allowing yourself to be mentally or verbally abused is unacceptable, too. Draw your mental, emotional, and spiritual boundaries as well. Dismiss any idea that is contrary to God's Word. Letting one person's negativity dictate your mental, emotional, or spiritual well-being is not healthy. His Word is the voice that matters. Confronting an individual who violates who you are in Christ is acceptable. Christ calls us to be humble and gentle, making "every effort to keep the unity of the Spirit through the bond of peace."[198]

Maintaining unity within Christian relationships can be tricky. Applied seniors are directed towards Jesus's words in Matthew 18:15-19,

> "If your brother or sister sins, go and point out their fault, just between the two of you. If they listen to you, you have won them over. But if they will not listen, take one or two others

---

[197] Acts 2:42-27

[198] Ephesians 4:2-3

> along, so that 'every matter may be established by the testimony of two or three witnesses.' If they still refuse to listen, tell it to the church; and if they refuse to listen even to the church, treat them as you would a pagan or a tax collector.

Excommunication, the final step, is not an act of hate but of love. Sin separates us from God. Sin, therefore, is not to be tolerated by anyone. Refusing to acknowledge one's sinfulness places them in great spiritual danger. Congregations that excommunicate members do so to bring awareness to the egregiousness of sin. Best case scenario, the individual recognizes their sin, repents, and is welcomed back into fellowship. In the context of Applied's discussion, separation from a friend who refuses to acknowledge their sinful influence protects both the believer and the unrepentant. Our act of separation is intended to show our friend the seriousness of their action or attitude.

Mentioned earlier, separation is more a process than immediate action. Jesus's first step in Matthew 18 insists on a face to face conversation. Instead of accepting your friend's frat party invitation, invite them elsewhere while gently rebuking their sinful action. If they continue to walk in sin and refuse assistance by you and your other friends, little can be done. Refusal is their decision and so too are the consequences. Assistance is not to be refused when your friend comes knocking for help, but, "Do not be yoked together with unbelievers. For what do righteousness and wickedness have in common? Or what fellowship can light have with darkness?"[199]

Discerning students raise the question, "How can we do this without being judgmental?" Avoiding a judgmental attitude is possible. It requires humility, gentleness, patience, and perspective.[200] A perspective that centers on the cross, recognizing no one is a good person and all need Christ.[201]

Maintaining this perspective and humility requires maturity and growth. Remembering that we too are sinners reminds us to be gentle in our approach. If sin is as serious as Scripture indicates, not holding each other accountable is foolish. Pointing ourselves and others towards the redeeming work of Christ is of priority.

---

[199] 2 Corinthians 6:14

[200] Ephesians 4:2-3

[201] Romans 3:10-11

Chapter 15

Influence of College: Maintaining and Developing Faith

At the beginning of the year, seniors are provided a questionnaire seeking to understand their starting positions. Question twelve asks, "What question(s) do you want answered by the end of the year?"

One of the most popular answers is, "How can I maintain my faith when I go to college?" My friends, stay rooted in Scripture, start, and start at the cross and watch your influences. Be aware.

After discussing friendships and boundaries, students are provided a list of mechanisms to further assist in staying rooted in Christ. College influences everyone, one way or the other. Individuals choose which way they will be influenced. Graduating seniors must be prepared for the transition as much as possible. "It's a whole new world, a dazzling place I [they] never knew, and if they are not careful, they can be quickly swept away." [202] How do we take the fight to college?

1. Get connected. Pay attention to the bulletin boards in your dorm and commons area. Look to see if there are any Bible studies being led by anyone on the floor. If none exist, make one.[203] Most colleges will have welcome weekends and orientations. Tables will be scattered in the quad with groups galore. Search out Christian groups and join. Humans were designed for fellowship. Hiding in your room is not a viable option. Search for God-pleasing fellowship once your room is set up, or even before you reach campus.
2. Find a local congregation *prior* to college. Time is carved out of class for students to go to www.lcms.org and search for the closest Lutheran Church-Missouri Synod congregation to their college.[204] Students who are not Lutheran Church-Missouri Synod members are provided instructions to find their area denominational congregation. After locating the congregation, students write the address of the local church in their notebook. No excuses.
3. Identify if the congregation has an active youth group that ministers to college students. Is it rooted in Word and

---

[202] If you are fortunate enough, you'll hear me sing this classic line from Aladdin.

[203] Shout out to the many Lutheran North graduates who have taken that initiative.

[204] Click on "Locators" then select "Find a church."

sacrament? Does the congregation preach Christ crucified, Christ risen, or is it more interested in making people good? Congregations may have this information posted on their webpage. Visiting the congregation and asking members is encouraged.

4. Using the Internet again, students search for on-campus Christian organizations such as CRU, InterVarsity, LCMS U or Ratio Christi.[205]
5. Applied binders contain not only resources, but Scripture verses and important insights shared in class. Taking their binder to college provides students a strong resource either for themselves or questioning roommate.[206] Of course, taking a physical copy of the Scriptures is expected as it is *the* resource.
6. Be intentional about maintaining the faith. Meditate on the Word of God daily. Find a reading plan that walks you through Scripture. You cannot go off to college and expect to grow as a Christian if you are not seeking opportunities to grow. Read Christian websites and books, journal, pray, and listen to Christian music. Students are confused when I say, "Don't make time for God." After a short pause, I continue with my point. Your faith is not something you do; it is who you are. Sure, meditating on the Word of God requires setting aside time. Do it. But the idea is to remember one's faith is not limited to Sunday morning. Being a Christian is different than "doing" Christianity. One approach leads you to the cross, the other threatens to lead you the other direction.
7. Stay structured. Develop God-pleasing habits and disciplines. Freedom is wonderful, but it carries significant vulnerabilities. Establish and follow a consistent sleep schedule. Physical health is connected to mental and emotional health. Exercise daily and find time to relax.
8. Most importantly and echoing above, mediate on the Word of God day and night and attend worship on a regular basis. Speak on it daily. Dwell within the Word. Pray continually. *Lean in*, taking the fight to college and do not get knocked down early in the first round. You control how you are influenced. Breathing in the Word of God daily assures an influence towards the cross. Partake of sacrament and be renewed weekly.

---

[205] Campus Apologetics Alliance

[206] *Applied Christianity: Worldview Training for the 21st Century Christian* contains most of what students write in their binders.

Part V

Dating and Relationships

Chapter 16

Tattoos, Piercings and Makeup

Makeup, tattoos, and piercings begin our conversation on dating and relationships. Perhaps an unusual beginning place for many but it makes sense when the full conversation is completed. Both genders are given a survey regarding their opinions on the trio. Young men answer questions related to ladies, and ladies answer questions regarding young men. Here are the questions:

Ladies:

1. Why do women wear makeup?
2. Do you wear makeup?
3. Why do you wear makeup?
4. Women who do not wear makeup are:
5. Ladies, do you wear earrings and other jewelry? Why?
6. Ladies, when you see a man wearing an earring(s), what are your initial thoughts?
7. Ladies, when you see a man with a tattoo, of anything, your initial thoughts are?

Men:

1. Do you wear makeup?[207]
2. Men, why do women wear makeup?
3. Why do women wear jewelry?
4. Men, ladies who wear jewelry are:
5. Ladies who do not wear makeup are:
6. Do you prefer women who wear makeup? Why/Why not?
7. Guys, when you see a woman with a tattoo, you think:

Reponses are read aloud in class. Answers from the men and women often echo. Ladies are usually harsher on themselves than what the young men are. The question, "Why does a woman wear makeup?" is answered "to be more confident," "cover up blemishes," "to feel better about themselves" or "because they don't like how they look." Like clockwork, every year a few young ladies answer, "I'm ugly" or "I

---

[207] A joke to keep the spirits up as the conversations are about to get deep.

don't like my face." Those types of answers bring to light that earrings and tattoos are not the true focus of our conversation. We spend a few minutes unpacking various answers from both perspectives. Both genders share insights and, sometimes, insecurities.

They are applauded for their maturity. We are talking about dating, relationships, and marriage. Last time I checked, open communication and listening to your spouse was of utmost importance. Topical conversations are almost always eclipsed by a greater purpose. As you will find out, I could care less about makeup. Deeper issues need to be addressed, including effective communication. Healthy back and forth conversation are met with another teacher prompt that seeks to illuminate the greater purpose behind questions.

"Why won't my daughter be wearing makeup?"

Eyes open a bit wider and I see a few heads shaking in pre-mature disappointment. Assumptions are not always wise. Students are encouraged to avoid jumping to conclusions. Senior girls ask expected questions, "She won't ever be allowed to wear makeup, or until she's out of the house?" Or, "What about homecomings?" "Does your wife wear makeup?"[208] I explain that if my daughter were to ask me if she could wear makeup, I would listen to hear reasoning.

Insightful students inquire, "What reason could she give that you would say yes?" Bad answers are obvious, "Everyone else is doing it," and, "I'm ugly without it." One legit reason could be, "I've never done makeup, Dad. I want to see what it's like." Why would I care? Knock yourself out, kid. We will talk about her experience later. Did you like it? Was it fun? Is it something you want to do more? Why? Depending on how much time remains in class, this back and forth could last a while, but concludes the same every year:

> "Listen," I say, "I could care less if you wear makeup. I only care that my daughter (and you) knows who she is and whose she is in Christ. If she wants to wear makeup because "she's ugly" or, "everyone else is doing it," it won't fly. Her value and identity in Christ must be priority. Assuming these two points of emphasis are believed and practiced, permission granted.

Twenty years in the classroom has given me ample opportunity to see young men and women broken to the core. Comparing themselves to each other, past girlfriends, and hour-glass models glorified in the

---

[208] No.

media is doing more harm than good. As a parent, my responsibility is to lead my children to the cross, not the expectations of the world.

Unless the reader missed it, wearing makeup is the least of my concerns. I only care that you know who you are and whose you are, a point repeated multiple times as the period ends and throughout the year, really.

Men, how important is the external appearance of women? Women, how important is the external appearance of men, and yourself? Are we going to base a relationship on physical appearances? If someone has a tattoo, are we going to ignore their existence? They have a nose ring or two, or five, does this disqualify them from your time? Applied's makeup, tattoo, and piercing conversation is a catalyst for raising multiple points:

1. Know who you are and whose you are in Christ.[209]
2. Your value, identity, and purpose (VIP) are found in Christ, not the world.
3. I am glad that both the young men and women are not shallow enough to hold one's looks against the opposite sex. Men and women are more than physical objects to be lusted after.

Whether they remain consistent in elevating internal beauty above external beauty is to be determined later in the unit.[210]

Excitement increases as we near the tattoo conversation. Role playing introduces the topic, "Today, I am your dad. Convince me to allow you to get a tattoo."

Fireworks are not my cup of tea, but this conversation sets a few off…in my direction. By now, students already know to ask questions instead of settling for statements. "Dad, *why can't* I have a tattoo?" a student may ask, putting the proverbial ball back in my court.

Expecting their question, I return their volley, "Scripture says do not put tattoo marks on your body. Any other questions?" Astonishment and panic cover their faces. Deal breaker if true. If only they read Scripture they would not have to ask, "Where does it say that?" Lay-ups are too easy, "Leviticus 19:28. Ha." Newly discovered experts on systematic theology respond, "But that's the Old Testament."

---

[209] I rarely get emotional in class. In 2019, when reading the ladies' comments about themselves, I was heartbroken and moved to tears. It took me a few seconds to regain my composure. Shh, do not tell anyone, please.

[210] 1 Peter 3:3-6

Correct. So? Applying lessons learned in Old and New Testament classes would end the conversation if these students were the systematic theologians they suddenly claim to be.

If one recalls, in the Old Testament, priests would offer sacrifices to God on behalf of people. New Testament theology teaches that Jesus becomes both the priest and the sacrifice, voiding ceremonial law and a need for further sacrifices. Leviticus 19 no longer applies or carries weight in the conversation. Christians have freedom within the Gospel to get a tattoo. Freedom in Christ does not necessarily equate to freedom at home. Children are still expected to obey their parents, the authority entrusted to them by the Lord.[211]

Tattoos, like makeup are the least of my concerns.[212] Of primary importance is their understanding of Christ's work on the cross. Disobeying your parents equates to disrespect towards God.

Parents may not appreciate their child's boyfriend or girlfriend's tattoo, but it is not a deal breaker. Tattoos, piercings, and makeup are one part to a larger conversation on who and whose we are in Christ. God's ownership of His creation impacts our dating relationships. *Who you* are matters just as much if not more than who you are going to date.

Which is why Applied students take Florence Littauer's personality survey.[213] Knowing who you are and how you operate influences your ability to relate and communicate with your spouse-and your soon to be college roommates. Having established each student's personality style, they work in partnerships and apply their personalities to college life.

Watching the social dynamic of each personality partnership is entertaining. Powerful Cholerics like controlling the situation. Perfect Melancholy and Peaceful Phlegmatics are introverted individuals who may be more than happy to let the Choleric rule. Will the Choleric dominate or manipulate the conversation? Extroverted Popular Sanguines thrive on attention. In groups and partnerships, they tend to do the talking and not always on task. Imagine the Powerful Choleric who seeks mission accomplishment working with a Popular Sanguine, who for the third time is recalling their weekend antics.

---

[211] Ephesians 6:1-4

[212] There are weaker and less effective arguments against tattoos. Challengers may argue that a tattoo is harming the temple of God. So too is drinking an addictive substance like coffee or working out in the weight-room where muscles are literally torn, or perhaps, eating unhealthy food or drinking too much alcohol. Legalism is not to be equated with the Gospel of Christ.

[213] *Personality Plus*

In only a few months, students will be faced with a new environment and multiple roommates of different personalities. Perfectionist will share rooms with individuals whose closet is the floor and bed. Popular Sanguine's may be partnered with a Peaceful Phlegmatic who just wants to do their homework without listening to their new "friend" blabber. Awareness of your personality style can aid in the transition to college. Making friends will not be difficult for the Popular Sanguine who loves to chat and be the center of attention. Finding God-pleasing friends that lead them to the cross will be the challenge. Social activities are not to compromise their moral and spiritual lines. Their strength is also their weakness. Awareness is key. Peaceful Phlegmatics are not off the hook. Quiet and reserved, Peaceful Phlegmatic may be content to hide in the dorm. Considering the transition from high school to college is mentally and emotionally strenuous, hiding in the room may be literal. Hiding in fear will not aide a healthy college transition. Knowing yourself and how you operate will help your transition. High school was easy. Now the real work begins.

I am a Powerful Choleric, an extroverted individual who seeks mission completion. Mrs. Horvath is a Peaceful Phlegmatic. She is an introverted woman who is thoughtful and patient. Mrs. Horvath will watch my flailing attempts at mission completion and wait to help, when needed. We are two different personalities, but we share a common belief: Who we are and whose we are is found in Christ. Neither of us have tattoos, piercings, or wear makeup.[214] External attributes matter little when compared to the inner beauty of Christ and a larger perspective. Our strengths and weaknesses are known by both and knowing is half the battle.[215] The second half is recognizing our strengths and weaknesses and finding practical and loving methods of co-existing-not only with each other but also with our children who may have different personality styles.

I like seeing students embrace the personality conversation. Guys and girls can be seen taking copies of the survey home to their parents, boyfriends or girlfriends that attend other high schools. Girlfriends and boyfriends see their partners and themselves in a new light. Knowing how to communicate and exist within relationships can save marriages and friendships.

---

[214] If you were paying attention, you know that I am *not* saying that those who have tattoos, piercings or wear make-up do not have the inner beauty of Christ. I…do not…care if you have the trio, so long as you know who and whose you are.

[215] Few students catch this 1980's cartoon reference.

Personality surveys are important enough to use in career searching as well. College majors and careers need to be selected before graduation. Unnecessary pressure mounts from parents and outsiders to declare their lifelong major and career before graduating high school. Adding to the plate is the notion that God has a secret plan not yet decoded or discovered. It is no wonder why youth depression and anxiety levels are skyrocketing. Society is directing our youth in the wrong direction. Matching a personality style with a career provides students with options not yet considered. Extroverted Popular Sanguine's may not appreciate a lifelong career in a cubicle. Introverted Peaceful Phlegmatics' may not appreciate a career in hospitality.

Littauer's survey is fun *and* important. God has granted each of us unique gifts, talents, and abilities. Identifying who we and what those gifts are can help create and maintain healthy relationships and careers; careers that place us in opportunities to be the masks of God as we love Him, love His people, and share the Gospel.

Chapter 17

Are they the *one?*

Introspection is a life-changer. Mark Divine's previous words ring true, "By defining your stand and purpose, you will be able to use them as an internal GPS. When the winds of pain and pleasure blow, you won't change course."[216] Knowing your value, identity, and purpose gives you answers and direction. Maintaining a Christ-centered point of view is clutch.[217] When the pressures, pain, and pleasures of college (life) present themselves, you already know how to react.

Seniors, and even some grown adults, may protest a theological or ethical position by stating, "You won't know what you will do until you are in that situation." False. Forward thinking, and planning saves you from relying on unplanned and erratic emotional responses and unnecessary consequences. Walking into a party and witnessing underage drinking or alcohol abuse is not a, "I won't know what to do until I'm in the situation," scenario. A Christian's worldview leads to an easy solution: walk back out the door.

Diving head-first into college is not prudent. Mistakes can be avoided. Pastor Marcus Zill of LC-MS U proposes a college student's responsibility is to maintain their faith, earn their diploma and find a spouse. Student's faith life is priority one followed by academics, but I encourage students to not force relationships. Finding a spouse in college may be typical but not required. Relax. Stay rooted in Christ and focus on your education. Romantic relationships are inevitable though, and after securing who and whose we are in Christ, our conversation shifts to contemplating characteristics of an ideal spouse.

Prompt:

> Seniors create your top ten list. Who do you want your spouse to be?

Four or five minutes is long enough for an individual to make a list of ten items. For this unit, I like partnering young men and women together for another five minutes with the assignment of combining their list of twenty to one list of ten.

Relationships require communication and compromise. With step one completed, step two begins. Then we combine two partnerships, each with their own, reduced lists. Now, the four must take their two

---

[216] *The Way of the Seal.*

[217] Students cringe when I use 80's language.

lists and reduce it again to one list of ten items. Now we have four students discussing their opinions on significant spousal characteristics.

Each student has their own perspective. Communicating with other students may present a perspective not considered on their own. Maybe at the end of the conversation, students do not change their perspective and are solidified in their original lists. Or, they may change their original thinking dramatically, based on what other students say.

Step three combines two more partnerships into our mix. Eight teenagers begin discussing the most important characteristics of the opposite sex. Intermingling groups according to personality styles makes eavesdropping entertaining. Applied's average class size is twenty-eight per period. When all is said and done, we have three larger groups and three lists. Representatives from each group write their list on the whiteboard at the front of the room.

Lists have become less superficial over the years. Consequently, conversation has shifted from being mostly just entertaining and sometimes beneficial to mostly reflective, beneficial, and sometimes entertaining. Recent repeat top-ten characteristics that make the cut:

1. Christian (same worldview)
2. Trustworthy
3. Family Oriented
4. Driven
5. Attractive Personality
6. Similar Interest
7. Honest
8. Faithful
9. Diligent
10. Peaceful

Explanations of each characteristic tend to be consistent from one year to the next. Moral and spiritual lines make another appearance in our conversation on whether a Christian ought to marry an atheist. Topics such as baptism and education choices are obvious concerns for Christians who are considering marrying an atheist. Secular agendas that permeate education are different than a Christ centered education. Raising a child in the ways of the Lord is different than raising one rooted in secularism. What's your line? What's your destination? And will you be taking your children with you?

Physical attractiveness may be an initial conversation starter, but personalities tend to last longer than outward appearances.

Pregnancies, full time jobs and a host of other reasons influence the outside appearance, male or female.

Days after selecting and discussing their lists, I do the honor of presenting "my" list which comes from Proverbs 31:10-31and 1 Timothy 3:1-6.[218] *UnConformed*, my first book, discusses attributes of a godly leader found in 1 Timothy 3.

Men have been given a special responsibility of leading their families towards the cross. Though the unit is directed at both ladies and gentlemen, men are called out and encouraged to lead better. Growing up, I failed in high school, college and the first years of marriage. Wisdom comes through experience. You do not have to go through unnecessary experiences at the expense of other people's mental, emotional, physical, and spiritual well-being. Life is not only about you.

First, ladies create a top-ten list from 1 Timothy 3 while men create a list from Proverbs 31. Seeing their work completed earns more work as they switch passages repeating the process. Paul's list of qualifications for a godly overseer:

> Here is a trustworthy saying: Whoever aspires to be an overseer desires a noble task. Now the overseer is to be above reproach, faithful to his wife, temperate, self-controlled, respectable, hospitable, able to teach, not given to drunkenness, not violent but gentle, not quarrelsome, not a lover of money. He must manage his own family well and see that his children obey him, and he must do so in a manner worthy of full respect. (If anyone does not know how to manage his own family, how can he take care of God's church?) He must not be a recent convert, or he may become conceited and fall under the same judgment as the devil.

With lists completed, students find specific examples of each attribute. Being faithful to his wife means not looking at pornography or other women while "out with the boys." Temperate is rendered "vigilant" in the King James version, meaning a husband (overseer) ought to keep his eye open for possible threats to the family outside of the virtual gaming realm. Protecting the family from physical threats may seem more obvious than warding off "hollow and deceptive philosophy, which depends on human tradition and the elemental

---

[218] https://www.proverbs31.org/ is an excellent resource for women looking to remain rooted in Christ.

spiritual forces of this world rather than on Christ."[219]

Children follow the lead of their parents one way or another. Glorifying the world's practices and beliefs encourages our children to walk the same direction. Maintaining awareness becomes difficult when spiritually and physically intoxicated with the world. Spiritual intoxication leads the family away from Christ. Rooting one's family in Word and Sacrament detoxifies the soul.

Teaching the family not only includes setting a proper example in word and speech but also teaching God's Word. Neglecting worship, godly teachings, and practices reaps unwanted consequences for both parent and child.

Specific examples move the class beyond generalities. Being drunk is never supported in Scripture, only condemned. We know this already, but what does it look like in "real life?" High school seniors are only eighteen and are working with a limited perspective. Bumper to bumper traffic and sixty-hour work weeks (and more) for fifty weeks out of the year are not the norm for them, yet.

Parents cannot afford to lose their self-control or themselves in alcohol while being responsible for the mental, emotional, physical, and spiritual well-being of their family. Pastors, parents, and Christian leaders ought to think twice about making jokes about being intoxicated on Sunday or even the rest of the week. Impressionable young minds are paying attention. Christian leaders (or any Christian) that glorify or make light of anything prohibited in Scripture should remember the consequences for leading children into sin is harsh. Legal and responsible drinking is permitted in Scripture, abusing alcohol is forbidden.[220] [221]

Heading into college, my expectations for a spouse were superficial. Those who know my wife, know that Mrs. Horvath is anything but superficial. Students of Applied remember my characterization of myself in those early days as being a shallow person. Here is a good example: my main desire in a wife was one who was athletic and shared an interest in participating in sports. Shallow? Yes.

Mrs. Horvath offered(s) more important characteristics that I need. Raising children in the Lord is more important than raising them to be high-level athletes. Narrow-mindedness almost prevented me from

---

[219] Colossians 2:8

[220] According to the CDC, almost 100,000 alcohol related deaths happen every year. https://www.cdc.gov/alcohol/fact-sheets/alcohol-use.htm (I added 10,000 from accidents involving alcohol).

[221] Political point: Hypocritical are those that warn against gun violence which accounts for less than 15,000 murders per year but are silent about the life and death consequences of alcohol.

marrying the epitome of a Proverbs 31 woman.

My favorite Proverbs 31 verses which accurately describe my wife:

> She is clothed with strength and dignity; she can laugh at the days to come. She speaks with wisdom, and faithful instruction is on her tongue. She watches over the affairs of her household and does not eat the bread of idleness. Her children arise and call her blessed; her husband also, and he praises her: "Many women do noble things, but you surpass them all." Charm is deceptive, and beauty is fleeting; but a woman who fears the Lord is to be praised. Honor her for all that her hands have done, and let her works bring her praise at the city gate.[222]

Seductions of the world are enticing, yet often problematic and carry unfortunate consequences. Transitioning from high school to college introduces vulnerabilities never experienced nor even anticipated. Graduates will enjoy a level of freedom that is wonderful, but dangerous. Alone and isolated, students may leap into a relationship with the first boy or girl that fulfills their mental or emotional vacancy. Opening the door for unexpected physical intimacy that carries spiritual consequences and maybe physical consequences. Too fast, too soon. Do not conform to the patterns of the world. Relax.

Is he the *one?* Look over your shoulder as you run to the cross, which direction is he (or she) heading? Towards or away from Christ?

> Therefore, since we are surrounded by such a great cloud of witnesses, let us throw off everything that hinders and the sin that so easily entangles. And let us run with perseverance the race marked out for us, fixing our eyes on Jesus, the pioneer and perfecter of faith. For the joy set before him he endured the cross, scorning its shame, and sat down at the right hand of the throne of God.[223]

---

[222] Proverbs 31:25-31

[223] Hebrews 12:1-3

Chapter 18

The Dating Scene

Through more introspection we move from considering spousal attributes to peer into the dating scene. Several years ago, I was researching material for the unit and found Nathan Bailey's website that listed concerns and consequences of dating. Knowing it contradicts a secular approach to relationships made it an easy choice for a classroom activity. We make no distinction between going on a date and being in a committed relationship entering our conversation.

I ask the students to rate these statements on a scale of one to ten according to societal expectations.

Dating[224]...

1. leads to intimacy but not necessarily to commitment.
2. tends to skip the "friendship" stage of a relationship.
3. often mistakes a physical relationship for love.
4. can cause discontentment with God's gift of singleness.
5. develops a self-centered, feeling-oriented concept of love.
6. promotes lust and moderate sexual activity, opening the door for fornication.
7. creates a standard of comparison by which mates are first chosen, but after marriage rejected.
8. lacks the protections and guidance afforded by parental involvement of courtship.

In all, we discuss twenty statements from Bailey's webpage. Per our usual routine, seniors are expected to respond first on their own before coming together for larger class discussion. Restlessness is running high as the school year is nearing an end. Prom-proposals fill up social media posts. Boyfriends and girlfriends are making weekend and summer plans. Timing for the discussion is near perfection.

Of priority is widening the soon to be graduates' understanding of their upcoming transition. Dating in a secular society differs than it does in a Christian high school. Take number two as an example. High school relationships are traditionally born out of initial friendships created at lunch tables, athletic events, or shared classes. Johnny saw Julie in Math and Theology class and at the football game. Later in the week, John and Julie are working on a project together. Going to Sadie

---

[224] http://polynate.net/books/courtship/

Hawkins together makes sense. Months later, John and Julie are a couple, but only after seeing each other every day, eight hours a day, for months. Friendship, albeit out of convenience, was the foundation for their romantic relationship.

Adult paradigms tend to look different. College relationships may begin with long term friendships, but that is not always the case. Whereas in high school, John and Julie were in the same building for eight hours a day, now they must go out of their way to meet up after Philosophy 101. This is just one example out of many illustrating how things are different in college versus in high school.

Along those lines, we fail to consider are the multiple vulnerabilities associated with college that are absent in high school. High school students have direct access to established friendships, parental influence, and daily disciplines that provide positive structure and discipline. Experienced college students will tell you that college lacks the presence of parents and long-term friendships that began in kindergarten. Structure and discipline exist for those who seek it out intentionally. In college, three meals a day and a sleep schedule are considered luxuries.

I worry about the mental, emotional, physical, and spiritual transition that awaits graduating seniors. Justifiable excitement from looking into the future fills the classroom. It is a new ball game and awareness is key to making a successful transition. A young man or woman who is mentally, emotionally, socially, and spiritually vulnerable may find comfort in romantic advances of a new acquaintance. Physicality does not equate to love (see #3 from the list). Alone and isolated (lacking established friendships, parental influence, daily disciplines, etc.), it becomes easier for their moral and spiritual red line to blur or be erased. Slow down!

Each statement discussed in class triggers personal experiences which keeps the class entertained while humbling me. My experience is by no means unique and if students can learn from my stupidity, more power to those who listen. Wednesday of the first week of my first year in college was when I met Mrs. Horvath. Monday of the next week we were a dating couple. Too fast!

True, we are married now, but that does not mean there were not obstacles and difficulties that would have been avoided if a friendship rooted in Christ had come first. We were fortunate in how things played out. Many are not.

Number eight triggers an awkward story of parental involvement that offers class amusement and horror. I was a freshman in college and had been dating my mother-in-law's daughter for a couple months. Sunday worship was at 8am. Coming home from church, we found ourselves on the couch "spooning" while watching television in the basement.

My wife's mother did the old 'check the laundry trick.' Within seconds she had a basket worth of clothes and had made her way back upstairs, calling her daughter upstairs. I was oblivious. If I was in trouble for merely laying on the couch with her daughter, I was guilty, but was it that big of a deal? Minutes went by…and then…it was my turn. There in the living room we sat, my future mother-in-law, my girlfriend (now wife), and myself—nervous, but not sure why. On the table in front of us was a porcelain bowl.

My future mother-in-law began to talk about my going into the pastoral ministry and the image one projects.[225] Even the slightest "chip in the bowl" denigrated the purity and perfection of the bowl. Pre-marital sex disqualifies one from being "above reproach."[226] Parishioners would find it difficult to hear God's Word from a non-practicing Christian.

Retelling the story shocks secular-minded students. Imagine my shock being in that situation. Questions shoot out from every corner, "Do you get along with your mother-in-law?" Of course. I applaud her moral and spiritual courage broaching the conversation and her willingness to direct us towards Christ. Many young men and women distance themselves and their relationships from their parents, turning their backs on years of wisdom, insight, and guidance.

Stories can be entertaining, but the goal is to make them informative and instructive. "Consider your relationships," the seniors are instructed, "how did they begin and what will be your approach in college? Your future will be influenced by your process." Married, and leading two kids in Christ, does not happen by chance. It requires work and a perspective rooted in Christ. Re-evaluating our dating paradigm and placing it in the context of college is beyond beneficial. It is life changing.

College is messy with a variety of different temptations and vulnerabilities. Societal patterns and practices are warned against because they are rooted in sin and usually carry unfortunate consequences, some of which are irreversible. Compromising ourselves mentally, emotionally, physically, and most importantly spiritually, can be avoided if we know who we are, what we believe,

---

[225] My second major, social work being the first.

[226] *UnConformed* and 1 Timothy 3

why we believe what we do, and what our worldview looks like manifested.

Students rebut, "We need to date to find out what we want in a spouse." Not true. I know it is not true, because part two of the unit directly asked students to list spousal characteristics. We want kind, loving, mature, family oriented, and Christ-centered spouses who share our values. Dating is not required to know what we want or to find out if a person possesses those qualities. Dissatisfied, they respond, "What are we supposed to do then, not date?"

Dating is not discouraged, *per se*. The point we are driving at is that instead of rushing into relationships, a better method is to first establish friendships, then cautiously progress into a dating relationship that has a specific purpose that does not compromise who and whose we are in Christ.

Observe the potential spouse's behavior and attitudes in a variety of contexts. Christ-centered character, or a lack of, will become evident. Watch your new friend play sports or observe their reactions to bumper to bumper traffic. Invite your friend to a birthday party with ten five-year-old children. Developing the friendship over time, instead of jumping into a romantic relationship immediately, can prevent one from crossing one's physical and spiritual lines. Maybe the two-year relationship fails, but at least they did not sacrifice who and whose they are in Christ in the process.

Which is why at the beginning of our dating and relationship unit, I place a full can of Mountain Dew in front of the classroom that has an index card underneath that reads, "I am sex." If dating "promotes lust and moderate sexual activity, opening the door for fornication," we need to identify what sex is and is not. How far is too far?[227] What does it look like to give parts of ourselves away at great expense? The pop can opens the door for a conversation that can be a bit sketchy with seniors who are suffering from senioritis.

With a partner, the students are asked to find metaphors or analogies that connect the can of pop to sex. Common responses include,

1. It's tempting.
2. It's addicting.
3. Sharing "cans" encourages STI's[228]
4. Once it's open, it's open.

---

[227] Students that graduated prior to 2019 may remember an entertaining video on backrubs. The account associated with the video has been terminated.

[228] Sextually Transmitted Infections.

Shaming, as you will see, is not part of the conversation. My primary focus remains on the concept that whatever you give away, you cannot get back. I address this in *UnConformed:*

> Consider this scenario. Let's say you and a girl in high school have been dating a few months, and by 'dating' we just mean holding hands and passing notes. Well, as can be expected, things begin to progress. Finding yourselves alone one night, you exchange massive amounts of saliva. It was a harmless make out session, right? She will never have that "first kiss" again. Shouldn't that have been something her future husband ought to have had, which can now never be given back? Stretching our imagination to see further implications is not needed. Oral sex? Full intercourse? If you engage in these activities with a girl, you are taking that part of her sexual purity away from her. You cannot give it back to her. Was she a virgin? Not anymore. You took it from her. These are gifts that were meant for someone else which she is no longer able to give. The problem is compounded once you leave her life. Now when she begins other relationships, she has to have that awkward conversation with her other boyfriends. Or, years later she will have to tell her future husband of her past experiences, which you will be a part of, and perhaps your name will even come up. But kids will be kids, right? What you take away from a young lady, whether it's the first kiss or her first time doing 'x' (touches included), you can never give back. At the same time, your sexual purity 'bowl' is being 'chipped.' The last thing you want to be carrying around is lots of sexual experiences with lots of different women. This will be baggage that you will regret having to carry.

Male or female, when it comes to sexuality, whatever we give or take from another person, we cannot get or give back.

Most students are willing to consider holding hands and kissing innocuous behaviors. The impacts on one's romantic and sexual purity in those contexts are considered dinky. Fair enough. Advocating for current relationships to be abandoned is unrealistic.[229] Encouraging moral and spiritual prudence is the priority. Our Christian worldview recognizes that a member of the opposite sex is made in the image of God. Christian stewardship reminds us that our significant other belongs to the Lord and not to us. Keep your hands off her, or him. She (he) does not belong to you. Whatever you take from her, or him, you

---

[229] Nor is it done.

cannot give back. Lead differently.

Sex is meant for the marital union and only the marital union, "That is why a man leaves his father and mother and is united to his wife, and they become one flesh."[230] Secular individuals would find that Scripture absurd and non-sensical. Statistics bear out that society's secular, have fun but be safe, approach does more harm than good. Relationships require, whether intentional or not, mental, emotional, physical, and spiritual investment. Preventing unnecessary hurt seems like a good plan of action.

Defining love becomes imperative. "Love is not love," as we are told by the world. Sex is not love. Sex is an expression of love between two individuals. 1 John 4 provides a proper definition of love,

> And so we know and rely on the love God has for us. God is love. Whoever lives in love lives in God, and God in them. This is how love is made complete among us so that we will have confidence on the day of judgment: In this world we are like Jesus… We love because he first loved us. Whoever claims to love God yet hates[231] a brother or sister is a liar. For whoever does not love their brother and sister, whom they have seen, cannot love God, whom they have not seen. And he has given us this command: Anyone who loves God must also love their brother and sister.

Our question is not "What is love?"[232] but "*Who* is love?" Love is not an emotional or chemical reaction or a feeling you get when you are around someone. Those are called hormones. God is love. Love is found in the world because God created the world and God is love. Where is love found in the atheistic worldview?

> In a universe of electrons and selfish genes, blind physical forces and genetic replication, some people are going to get hurt, other people are going to get lucky, and you won't find any rhyme or reason in it, nor any justice. The universe that we observe has precisely the properties we should expect if there is, at bottom, no design, no purpose, no evil, no good, nothing but pitiless indifference.[233]

Secularism encourages young men and women to have fun "but be safe." Condoms are placed in high school bathrooms. Olympic athletes

---

[230] Genesis 2:24

[231] Another opportunity to discuss racism and forgiveness.

[232] Obligatory response, "Baby don't hurt me…no more."

[233] Richard Dawkins, *River Out of Eden,* page 133

are provided condoms as needed. Hollywood glorifies sex, condemning those who seek to uphold its sacredness.

Millions of teens and adults have listened more to secular society and their hormones and have crossed the line. One flesh unions have been distorted and damaged. What is one to do?

Without hesitation and a tone of seriousness, students are reminded of Romans 8:1-2, "Therefore, there is now no condemnation for those who are in Christ Jesus, because through Christ Jesus the law of the Spirit who gives life has set you free from the law of sin and death." Boyfriends and girlfriends are encouraged to return to their partners and discuss redrawing their moral and spiritual lines, "Let's lead each other differently." Redemption, not shame, answers our question, "What now?"

For those who have not crossed that line, the reminder to hold firm rings loud and clear even as the classroom remains dead silent.

Our dating and relationship unit does not include lengthy conversations on marriage other than the above examples. Discussions on marital finances or negotiating whose house to go to for CHRISTmas are left for their future spouse. Applied does the leg work leading up to marriage. Work that begins in our first unit on God's existence and our worldview.

If God exists, God is responsible for the creation of the world. If God is responsible for the creation of the world, He is responsible for His creations. Humans are God's creations. If humans are God's creation, men and women belong to God. We are more than evolved animals with hormones. We are image bearers of the Creator. Designed to join in one flesh unions. Therefore, entering dating relationships should be done so with great meaning and purpose. Seeking to protect God's image which resides in His creation,

> Now as the church submits to Christ, so also wives should submit to their husbands in everything. Husbands, love your wives, just as Christ loved the church and gave himself up for her to make her holy, cleansing her by the washing with water through the word, and to present her to himself as a radiant church, without stain or wrinkle or any other blemish, but holy and blameless. In this same way, husbands ought to love their wives as their own bodies.[234]

[234] Ephesians 4:24-28

Chapter 19

Distortions of God's Intentions Homosexuality and Divorce

Perhaps the most sensitive topic of the year is also one that is widely accepted but not often researched, homosexuality. Knowing some students to be gay makes our conversation emotionally and mentally draining. Relationships that I have spent years developing may become strained. Society is guilty of convincing the world that possessing a gay orientation is part of God's plan. Reappearing into the conversation is the question, "Why do people care so much about what Christians believe?" Political progressives argue that Christians are hindering the advancement of society by opposing homosexuality.

Our conversations on influence, personal development in college, and dating, takes more time every year. Applied used to spend a week discussing homosexuality, but it ran into time constraints and, again, it was draining. Varying from one year to the next, the conversation has been reduced to one or two days. Our first task evaluates Scripture that allegedly supports homosexuality. Second, we place those passages in their proper context showing Scripture does not support or encourage gay relationships.

Ruth and Naomi are favorite examples of an alleged lesbian relationship in the Scriptures.

> But Ruth replied, "Do not urge me to leave you or to turn back from you. Where you go I will go, and where you stay I will stay. Your people will be my people and your God my God. Where you die I will die, and there I will be buried. May the LORD deal with me, be it ever so severely, if even death separates you and me." When Naomi realized that Ruth was determined to go with her, she stopped urging her.[235]

From this we are to conclude Ruth and Naomi were lesbians! Applied addresses the context of Ruth's and Naomi's relationship:

> With her two daughters-in-law she left the place where she had been living and set out on the road that would take them back to the land of Judah. Then Naomi said to her two daughters-in-law, "Go back, each of you, to your mother's home. May the LORD show you kindness, as you have shown kindness to your

[235] Ruth 1:16-22

> dead husbands and to me. May the LORD grant that each of you will find rest in the home of another husband." Then she kissed them goodbye and they wept aloud and said to her, "We will go back with you to your people." But Naomi said, "Return home, my daughters. Why would you come with me? Am I going to have any more sons, who could become your husbands? Return home, my daughters; I am too old to have another husband. Even if I thought there was still hope for me—even if I had a husband tonight and then gave birth to sons— would you wait until they grew up? Would you remain unmarried for them?[236]

Catch it? Naomi was married to Elimelek. Ruth was married to their *son.* Naomi was Ruth's mother-in-law. Ruth's husband died. Naomi reminded Ruth that she was of an age that getting re-married and conceiving another son was improbable. Naomi says, "May the LORD grant that each of you will find rest in the home of another husband." Go back to your "mother's home," are Naomi's instructions, and marry another husband. No part of this context implies a lesbian relationship, let alone a bisexual relationship. Ruth's husband had died. Staying with her mother-in-law made more sense than going home and trying to find another husband. She should be commended for her commitment, not used as a political pawn thousands of years later.

Jonathan and David are another Scripture pair used to support homosexuality. Again, the context of their relationship within Judaism fails to support the pro-homosexual agenda. Kevin DeYoung's, *What Does the Bible Really Teach about Homosexuality?* addresses the topic according to God's Word. Any work, *Applied Christianity* included, that wishes to address homosexuality, is obligated to begin at creation as found in Genesis.

School years begin with mandatory summer meetings, some requiring more traveling than others. One year, I left myself enough time to be at least thirty minutes early to a meeting an hour away.[237] Fail. Traffic was worse than expected. Pouring rain had slowed downtown Detroit traffic to a crawl. What was supposed to be a sixty-minute trip turned into a two and a half-hour nightmare.

Our annual meetings start with a worship service led by an area pastor. Catching the tail end of the message I heard, "distortion of Genesis." While the superintendent was commenting on the never-ending healthcare changes that affected our association, I read Genesis

---

[236] Ruth 1:7-13a

[237] Early is on time, and on time is late.

1 and 2, looking for ways in which the world had distorted Genesis. These are my thoughts, not the pastor's.

God's creation as found in Genesis has been distorted in at least five ways:

1) Genesis 1:1, "In the beginning God created the heavens and the earth."

   a. God does not exist. Man is the ultimate authority.
   b. The big bang explains the origins of the universe.

2) Genesis 1:26, "Then God said, "Let us make mankind in our image, in our likeness, so that they may rule over the fish in the sea and the birds in the sky, over the livestock and all the wild animals, and over all the creatures that move along the ground."

   a. Man is nothing but an evolved animal, no different than those that move along the ground.
   b. Evolution is responsible for who we are and where we came from.

3) Genesis 1:27, "So God created mankind in his own image, in the image of God he created them; male and female he created them."

   a. Gender is fluid, not determined.
   b. Identity, value and purpose is found in the image man creates for himself.

4) Genesis 2:24 "That is why a man leaves his father and mother and is united to his wife, and they become one flesh."[238]

   a. Marriage is not reserved for man and women, but for anyone who wishes to marry anyone or anything.
   b. Sex is pro-creative act that advances one's genome.

5) Genesis 3 records the sinful fall of man, consequences for sin and the solution to sin.

   a. Sin does not exist in a secular worldview, therefore there are no consequences and subsequently, no need for a savior.

---

[238] Spiritually and physically as echoed in Scripture (1 Corinthians 6; Ephesians 5).

Betraying the totality of Scripture, there are those that argue that Scripture only condemns sexual immorality and not committed homosexual relationships. Man's authority has replaced God's because, in the view of many, God does not exist. Man teaches we can behave according to our wants and desires without consequence, marrying and engaging in sexual relations with whomever. God's paradigm is much different, "That is why a man leaves his father and mother and is united to his wife, and they become one flesh."

Together the one flesh unions procreate and works the land entrusted by the Lord.[239] God's natural order for marital relationships is assumed from start to finish. God never prescribes homosexuality or polygamy in His Word.[240] He prescribes heterosexuality. His Word describes the corruption and distortion of His creation because of sin. Paul's letter to the Romans makes this clear as he systematically argues mankind's need for a savior.

Romans Chapter 1 lays the foundation of God's creation and its corruption:

> For since the creation of the world God's invisible qualities—his eternal power and divine nature—have been clearly seen, being understood from what has been made, so that people are without excuse. For although they knew God, they neither glorified him as God nor gave thanks to him, but their *thinking* became futile and their foolish hearts were darkened. Although they claimed to be wise, they became fools and exchanged the glory of the immortal God for images made to look like a mortal human being and birds and animals and reptiles. Therefore God gave them over in the sinful *desires* of their hearts to sexual impurity for the degrading of their bodies with one another. They exchanged the truth about God for a lie, and *worshiped* and served created things rather than the Creator—who is forever praised. Amen.[241] [Emphasis added]

Above we read that sin distorted godly worship, thoughts, desires, and actions. Mankind dismissed worshiping the Creator and worshiped themselves. Desires of the flesh became corrupt against the natural order of God's intended plan. Distorted desires and thoughts manifested themselves in distorted actions:

---

[239] Genesis 2:15-25

[240] Surrogacy was not part of his design, yet, he chose to work through the distortion as seen in Genesis 16.

[241] Romans 1:20-25

> Even their women exchanged natural sexual relations for unnatural ones. In the same way the men also abandoned natural relations with women and were inflamed with lust for one another. Men committed shameful acts with other men, and received in themselves the due penalty for their error.[242]

Take note, the distortion is the orientation and its manifestation, not the person. Heterosexuality was the intended plan, but homosexuality distorted God's created design. Sin corrupted the nature of the person, heterosexual or homosexual.

Paul elaborates in 1 Corinthians 6,

> "Or do you not know that wrongdoers will not inherit the kingdom of God? Do not be deceived: Neither the sexually immoral nor idolaters nor adulterers nor men who have sex with men nor thieves nor the greedy nor drunkards nor slanderers nor swindlers will inherit the kingdom of God."[243]

Our nature, Paul argues, is distorted. Distorted sinners are separated from Christ and need a savior. Which is why Paul follows verses nine and ten with, "And that is what some of you were. But you were washed, you were sanctified, you were justified in the name of the Lord Jesus Christ and by the Spirit of our God."[244] Scripture answers the question, "Can a homosexual be saved?" but I start by answering the question by asking another, "Can a heterosexual be saved?"

Christians are good at pointing out the sin of homosexuality while ignoring their own sins of sexual immorality, idolatry, drunkenness, slandering, or swindling. God's creation was good. Sex is good. Marriage is good. Man's distorted nature acted out in our lives is a misrepresentation of the pleasures created by God.

Being born a heterosexual sinner does not give me freedom to act sinfully. Doing so would be a violation and distortion of God's intentions. Recognizing my failures, I ask God to forgive my stupidity. He receives my plea giving His grace with the expectation that I sin no more. The same is true for the homosexual who recognizes their gay orientation fails to align with God's original intention. Living their orientation without recognizing it is a distortion is problematic; just as

---

[242] Romans 1:26-27

[243] 1 Corinthians 6:9-10

[244] The Corinthians were originally pagans who lived as they pleased. Men had sex with other men and/or they were adulterers who worshiped foreign gods. They put their trust in themselves and not in God. But being a Christian meant giving up pagan attitudes and behaviors, such as, men having sex with men, adultery, being greedy, and idolizing false gods.

much as the heterosexual who refuses to recognize their sexual immorality or drunkenness is a distortion.

Instead of getting drunk, we drink responsibly. Ceasing from fornication, we return to the cross. Idolizing athletes and movie stars should not replace worshipping God. Instead of acting on our distorted orientations, we remain celibate. A homosexual can be saved so long as they recognize their orientation is not aligned with God's intentions and do not act on their orientation.[245] Turning from sin is required from both the homosexual and heterosexual. Restated, we are *all* born sinners who are not allowed to sin boldly. Justified and sanctified in Christ becomes our mantra which is to be lived out in our lives.

Contrasting Paul with Jesus, students wonder whether Jesus opposed homosexuality. We open our Scriptures to address the secular claim Jesus never commented on homosexuality. First, Christians believe Jesus is God, the same God who is responsible for the creation of the world, and the same God who set the context of marriage and sexual relations to be between a man and a woman. If Jesus is God, and God is responsible for setting the context of marriage in the Old Testament, Jesus did not intend for gay marital relationships.

Second, Jesus was a religious Jew. He observed Jewish practices and teachings.[246] Responding to Pharisees who were attempting to trap him on Jewish divorce laws, Jesus replied,

> …at the beginning the Creator 'made them male and female,' and said, 'For this reason a man will leave his father and mother and be united to his wife, and the two will become one flesh'? So they are no longer two, but one flesh. Therefore what God has joined together, let no one separate.[247]

Jesus was the creator.[248] He created males and females to be united together in one flesh marital unions. Arguers are correct when they say Jesus does not say, "homosexual," anywhere in Scripture. Jesus's rebuke of the Pharisees clearly reiterates the creator of the world expected marriage to be between men and women. Third, arguing Jesus never condemned specific issues is poor reasoning. Jesus never specifically condemned polygamy, pedophilia, bestiality, drug use, or speeding on the highway. Does His silence imply acceptance? No way.

---

[245] The Internet contains plenty of individuals willingly remaining celibate due to following God. Dismissing them as fake and not sincere is misplaced.

[246] It amazes me that Christians believe Jesus was not religious. He was a practicing Jew who memorized Scripture and would have engaged in traditional worship practices.

[247] Matthew 19:4-6

[248] Colossians 1:15-27

What about the science?

Prior to examining Scripture and with one purpose in mind, students read Kelly Servick's 2015 article, "New Support for 'Gay Gene:' Replication of 1993 study highlights same region on X chromosome, but some still call evidence inconclusive."

The article directed the reader's attention to research linking homosexuality to a specific location on the X chromosome, Xq28. Promising results. But not everyone was convinced as Servick writes,

> Still, Sanders acknowledges that at least one journal rejected the work. And geneticist Neil Risch of the University of California, San Francisco, notes that the linkages Bailey and Sanders report do not rise to statistical significance. Risch collaborated on a 1999 study that found no association of homosexuality with Xq28.

As explained in more detail in class, Christians who wish to argue that it is impossible to be born gay are wrong. Those who argue that science has unequivocally proven people are born gay, and/or have a "gay gene," are also wrong. In fact, science is *not* settled on how someone may or may not be born gay. Acceptance of homosexuality was a moral and social decision made in the 1970s. Like abortion, the decision was not rooted in scientific discovery but in culture.

> The American Psychological Association supports the action taken on December 15, 1973, by the American Psychiatric Association removing homosexuality from that association's official list of mental disorders.[249]

As to the cause of homosexuality? The American Psychiatric Association believes that the causes of sexual orientation (whether homosexual or heterosexual) are not known at this time and likely are multifactorial including biological and behavioral roots which may vary between different individuals and may even vary over time.[250]

Reading the research that has been conducted in the last few decades leads me to agree with the APAs conclusion that there are multiple biological, environmental and epigenetic factors.[251] Epigenetic markers are "chemical changes to DNA that affect how genes are expressed but not the information they contain. These 'epi-marks' can be inherited

---

[249] https://www.apa.org/about/policy/discrimination.pdf

[250] APA Official Actions: Position Statement on Issues Related to Homosexuality, 2013

[251] Richard Horton's PBS article, *Is Homosexuality Inherited*? summarizes much of the science

but can also be altered by environmental factors."[252] There may be no gay gene, but it makes sense to me that an individual can grow up with a homosexual tendency that was created by biological, behavioral and environmental influences.

However, being born a homosexual does not equate to Biblical or moral justification. Evidence supports that genetics play a role in pedophilia,[253] psychopathy,[254] alcoholism,[255] etc. Society agrees these three are not to be encouraged or accepted morally, socially, or spiritually. No one is referring to homosexuals as pedophiles or psychopaths. What is being said is that there is enough science to conclude the "born this way" argument may not be wisest to make.

What is a Christian to do? Recognize society has determined homosexuality to be socially and morally acceptable. Speak the truth in love with gentleness and respect, and vote based on our citizenship in heaven, not on earth.

In 2000, a weekend trip found me visiting friends still attending Concordia University Wisconsin. Sleeping arrangements saw me sleeping on the small couch in the lounge. Morning came and standing above me was a friend of mine who is a homosexual. He leaned over and kissed me on the forehead, "Good Morning." Seasoned with gentleness and respect, I responded, "Good morning, John." Christians must improve on their social skills. True, aggressive secularism has further to go as they attempt to suppress ideas contrary to their movement, but Christians are,

> Christ's ambassadors; God is making his appeal through us. We speak for Christ when we plead, "Come back to God." For God made Christ, who never sinned, to be the offering for our sin, so that we could be made right with God through Christ.[256]

As in everything, Christians are to lead themselves and others to the foot of the cross where our heterosexual and homosexual sins are nailed to the cross.

---

[252] https://www.nature.com/news/epigenetic-tags-linked-to-homosexuality-in-men-1.18530
[253] https://www.ncbi.nlm.nih.gov/pmc/articles/PMC4393782/#R9
[254] https://www.ncbi.nlm.nih.gov/pubmed/27683227
[255] https://www.ncbi.nlm.nih.gov/pmc/articles/PMC2442454/
[256] 2 Corinthians 5:20-21

Divorce

Beginning our section on divorce, students are first asked to write down common reasons married couples are divorced. Having completed the simple task, their next assignment is to find Scripture supporting reasons for why married couples may divorce.

As an example, where does Scripture allow for divorce because the husband and wife no longer get along? Or, where does Scripture allow divorce for "falling out of love?" Spoiler alert, they are non-existent. Applied's activity carries two purposes, first to spark conversation and challenge the student's quick acceptance of divorce.

Second, to point the class towards God's purpose for marriage and the cross of Christ. Jesus's response to the Pharisees who were questioning Him on the legalities of divorce ended His with response, "So they are no longer two, but one flesh. Therefore, what God has joined together, let no one separate."[257] God uses the marital union of man and woman to point to His relationship with His creation, "For this reason a man will leave his father and mother and be united to his wife, and the two will become one flesh. This is a profound mystery—but I am talking about Christ and the church."[258] In Christ, the Creator becomes one with His creation. Malachi's words, "God hates divorce"[259] become more significant in this context.

God chose His people. He married himself to His creation, caring and providing for their every mental, emotional, physical, and spiritual need. The Israelites did not always fulfill their marital duty and committed spiritual adultery, divorcing themselves from the Lord.[260] This separation broke the Lord's heart. God, in His goodness, forgave His adulterous nation and has forgiven us. Christ's sacrifice on the cross once again reunited us to the Father. Whereas Jews worshipped in the temple, God dwells within His people, making them temples of God. Those of us in the Church are "one flesh" with the Lord. Who would in their right mind would divorce themselves from this relationship and violate this spiritual marriage by uniting it with sin?[261]

> Do you not know that your bodies are members of Christ himself? Shall I then take the members of Christ and unite them with a prostitute? Never. Do you not know that he who unites

---

[257] Matthew 19:6
[258] Ephesians 5:31-32
[259] Malachi 2:10-16
[260] Which is the context of Malachi 2
[261] Fornication included.

> himself with a prostitute is one with her in body? For it is said, "The two will become one flesh." But whoever is united with the Lord is one with him in spirit. Flee from sexual immorality. All other sins a person commits are outside the body, but whoever sins sexually, sins against their own body. Do you not know that your bodies are temples of the Holy Spirit, who is in you, whom you have received from God? You are not your own; you were bought at a price. Therefore honor God with your bodies.[262]

God's agony over our separation from Him resembles agony felt in divorce between husband and wife. Couples invest themselves mentally, emotionally, physically, and spiritually, giving everything of who and whose they are in Christ. Serious relationships that end, do so in great pain. Ever been dumped and felt like your heart was ripped out? Why? Because we gave all that we had in the relationship and it was for nothing. Marriage is more than sex, chemicals, and hormones. It is more than a contract at the courthouse. Marriage is the union of man and woman, who bear the image of God.

Man, or woman, is not to separate or infringe upon the one flesh union created in the eyes of the Lord, for any reason:

> Jesus replied, "Moses permitted you to divorce your wives because your hearts were hard. But it was not this way from the beginning. I tell you that anyone who divorces his wife, except for sexual immorality, and marries another woman commits adultery."[263]

Sexual immorality (adultery) would mean that a spouse took their one flesh union and violated it by uniting with another flesh. God's chosen people, the Israelites slipped into the same sin by abandoning God and worshiping a golden calf. How dare they unite with a foreign god? How dare we join our fleshes with another woman or man who is not our wife or husband? While adultery is a justification for divorce, it is not required. A just God could refuse reconciliation with His spiritual adulterers. Instead, He chose redemption and forgiveness. Marriage is to be honored by all and protected at all cost. Divorces in certain cases of abandonment and abusive relationships make sense.[264] An abusive and unrepentant spouse has all but deserted their vows. Even so, all divorce is a distortion of God's original intention for

[262] 1 Corinthians 6:15-20
[263] Matthew 19:8-9
[264] 1 Corinthians 7:8-16

marriage: the two becoming one flesh, let no one separate.

Divorces, tragic as they be, provide opportunities to work towards Christian reconciliation while pointing all parties involved to the reconciliation offered by Christ. Discussing who we are and what we want in spouse influences our conversation on divorce. Rushing into relationships rooted in lust during the initial weeks or months of college (or later) is *not* advisable. Marriages in America end half the time. Slowing relationships down, drawing moral and spiritual lines, and finding a spouse who lives their faith can lessen chances of ending up divorced. Relationships that start and operate according to the patterns of the world is not advisable for many reasons mentioned in Applied Christianity.

Starting and staying at the cross is advised.

Conclusion

May 29th, 2002 was the last day of my first year of teaching. I had survived. During 5th hour, soon to be graduate Kyle Krueger asked me, "Do you have a going away speech prepared?" I felt ashamed and embarrassed. Was I supposed to have one? It would make sense considering I would never see many of them again on this side of eternity. Failing to have any final words prepared, I apologized. To this date, nineteen years later, I still do not have an official going away speech prepared. Sort of.

On the last day of class, we conclude the way we began the year, listening to Switchfoot's, "Dare You to Move." Scanning the classroom, a few students can often be seen wiping away a tear or two.[265] Reality sets in as high school comes to completion. Not only that, many students have seen their friends every day for four or more years without fail, and this is about to end, too. Championships have been won and lost on the athletic field, courts, and trails. Dances and weekend slumber parties attended. Birthday celebrations shared. An end of an era has come.

While some may remain connected through college, others will not see each other again until eternity. As the song concludes, I stand in front of the students one last time. It is also the last time I will see many of them as they graduate and move onto life's next season.

I tell them about Kyle Krueger's question. I tell them I have no prepared speech. What else could I say on the last day of school that I have not already said during the school year? One-hundred-eighty days of Applied have been my going away speech. Constant and continual mental, emotional, physical, spiritual, academic, and social dares. Pokes and prods. Daily opportunities for self-introspection and growth.

Those who have ears to hear, let them hear.

In a similar fashion, *Applied Christianity: Worldview Training for the 21st Century Christian*, ends without an amazing conclusion. What else can I say that has not already been said in the previous pages?

Readers, like students, are reminded that my door is always open, except for when it is closed, and then you just have to knock. Perhaps, over the year, we had become dear to one another, so that as life moves into its next season, we can do so walking together, as opposed to me walking over you and you alone.[266]

Finishing my unofficial and unplanned speech (wink, wink) and for

---

[265] Or three, or four…

[266] 1 Thessalonians 2:8

one last time, the Gospel of Christ is preached. Ninety-nine percent of graduating seniors will not attend a Christian university. Chapel and theology classes will no longer be required. Hearing the Gospel of Christ on the last day of class may be the last time they hear how much Christ loves each and every one of them.

Briefly, we walk through the beginning of the year, starting with God's existence, moving to identifying our worldview, and then applying our foundation to life. All of this is useless if Christ did not resurrect from the dead. My new friends are reminded of the importance Christ's work:

> If there is no resurrection of the dead, then not even Christ has been raised. And if Christ has not been raised, our preaching is useless and so is your faith. More than that, we are then found to be false witnesses about God, for we have testified about God that he raised Christ from the dead. But he did not raise him if in fact the dead are not raised. For if the dead are not raised, then Christ has not been raised either. And if Christ has not been raised, your faith is futile; you are still in your sins.[267]

If Christ did not resurrect from the dead, our faith is futile. But if He *did* resurrect from the dead, then Christ is not a simple man like the rest of us. He is more than an example to live by in the community. Instead, a resurrected Christ

> is the image of the invisible God, the firstborn over all creation. For in him all things were created: things in heaven and on earth, visible and invisible, whether thrones or powers or rulers or authorities; all things have been created through him and for him. He is before all things, and in him all things hold together. And he is the head of the body, the church; he is the beginning and the firstborn from among the dead, so that in everything he might have the supremacy. For God was pleased to have all his fullness dwell in him, and through him to reconcile to himself all things, whether things on earth or things in heaven, by making peace through his blood, shed on the cross.[268]

Such a conclusion is astonishing as it provides a life changing perspective that begins at the cross: A Risen Christ means death and its

[267] 1 Corinthians 15:13-17
[268] Colossians 1:15-20

wages are defeated, your sins are forgiven, and you too shall be risen and united with Christ Himself, eternally.

There were many times in Applied Christianity where the use of an exclamation point was warranted. I get excited thinking about the opportunities and insights discussed in class. Applied's content offers students an opportunity to contemplate who they are, what they believe, why they believe it, and what their belief looks like manifested in every nook and cranny of life.

I implore them to have beliefs which are predicated upon the Lordship and resurrection of Christ.

Television and radio hosts often laud an athlete or actor's "unbelievable" performance. Yet, calling a diving catch "unbelievable" is hardly unbelievable. Obviously, when people say something is "unbelievable" they are commenting on how amazing and awesome it is. But we have seen hundreds if not thousands of diving catches and amazing performances by actors and actresses. Do you know what would be most amazing of all? Something that has only been done by just one person, with no good reason to think anyone else could ever do it, but with good reasons for thinking it did actually happen.

The Empty Tomb. The Resurrected Christ. Now *that* is "Unbelievable." It happened as much as it was needed in history: once. This is one "unbelievable" thing that you *can* believe in!

1st Century Christians recognized that the Risen Jesus was worthy of their worship and living as ambassadors of His amazing love, even to the point of death. Will you?

I dare you.

Intermission 3

Applied Christianity has been broken into six parts that do not reflect the true order of Applied. I have provided a table that juxtaposes the text with class.

Traditional Order of Instruction	**Order in this book, *Applied Christianity***
God's Existence	God's Existence
Worldview Introduction	Worldview Introduction
VIP Application	VIP Application is mixed in with God's Existence and worldview introduction
Ethical Issues: Sanctity of Life	Ethical Issues: Sanctity of Life
Historical Christianity: Gospel Authorship	Historical Christianity: Gospel Authorship
Influence Unit: Self, Friends and College	Historical Christianity: Manuscript Evidence
Historical Christianity: Manuscript Evidence	Historical Christianity: Books of the Bible
Historical Christianity: Books of the Bible	Historical Christianity: Contradictions/Archaeology
Influence: Self, Friends and College	Historical Christianity: Jesus and Non-Christians
Historical Christianity: Jesus and Non-Christians	Historical Christianity: The Resurrection
Dating and Relationships	Influence: Self, Friends and College
Ethical Issues: Homosexuality and Divorce	Dating and Relationships
Historical Christianity: The Resurrection	Ethical Issues: Homosexuality and Divorce

Part VI

Influential Class Videos And Appendixes

Part six of *Applied Christianity* documents favorite videos shown at the start of class and brief insights shared in Applied.

Switchfoot's, "Dare You to Move" acted as *Applied Christianity's* opening, and is therefore not represented below. Part six begins with day two of Applied. Having listened to Switchfoot the previous day and being 'dared to move', students are challenged to live for more than what the world has to offer, the Gospel.

Applied: Day 2

"Meant to Live", Switchfoot

Class Reflections:

Listening to "Meant to Live" recalls a question I asked seniors three years before when they were freshmen, "Why did you wake up today?" Answers are almost always the same, "To go to school." Depressing. Are we not meant to live for more than school, athletics, and careers? Near the middle of first quarter, worldview question seven will be connected to the question above, but on the second day of school, students are unaware of God's great purpose shared by His creation: Love God, love people, share the Gospel.

1) Losing ourselves in society and in our past is easy. Failed relationships and unfilled expectations leave lasting scars. Who we were meant to be is a long way off...if only there was a way we could start again: There is, at the foot of the cross.

2) Many students come into the classroom bent and broken. More teachers, in my opinion, should consider the untold stories each student brings into the classroom. Listening to anyone that believes students at a private Christian school live pretty perfect lives is offensive. Mental, emotional, and physical abuse are common. Death of a loved one, shameful pasts, divorces, abortions, addictions, broken families, family fights, alcoholism, and living paycheck to paycheck is far from perfect.

3) Christians were meant to live for more than what the world has to offer. Secular society cons Christians into accepting what it has to offer. Secularism is empty of substance. The desires and passions of the world, when lived from a secular point of view, leaves young men and women broken. In Christ, we were meant to live for more. We want more than what this world has to offer. How do we know this? We have seen what the world has been offering, and it is disappointing.

Applied: Day 3

"Courageous", Casting Crowns[269]

Class Reflections:

1. Generational influence can be changed if needed. If the pattern established by your parents is not a healthy pattern, change it. Break the chains and establish a new pattern for your family. Doing so will create a new pattern for your children and your children's children. To bolster my point, I call to the front a student or two that I know has a younger sibling or boyfriend/girlfriend. Putting them on the spot in front of their classmates, I challenge the student on the direction they are leading their sibling or partner. Are they leading their brother or sister towards Christ in the music they listen to or their weekend activities? *You* are impacting the eternal future of your siblings.
2. Fighting the good fight will take effort. Watching on the sidelines will not get the job done. Put the gaming remote down. Stop getting lost in your cellphone. Lead and live with purpose. Where do we start? At the redemptive work of Christ. A student is once again brought to the front of the classroom where they nervously stand with thirty sets of eyes on their every move. This is easy though. In front of the student are mostly friends or acquaintances. Within months, the student will be attending a state school consisting of forty-thousand or more students. Will they stand true to the Cross?
3. Humility and submission are required of us all as we stand before Christ. As the lyrics state, "The only way we'll ever stand is on our knees with lifted hands." Christians are called to live His purpose as opposed to our own. Try convincing a graduating high school senior that the King's purpose is more liberating than the freedom found at the state school hours away from their parents. Freedoms offered in college and society only shackle the Christian to the world.
4. Self-reflection begins in the mind and heart, and manifests into action. Students can be seen laughing and staring at me as I drive the point home by repeating four or five times the line, "In the war of the mind—I will make my stand—In the battle of the heart—And the battle of the hand."[270] Do they get it, though? Satan wants our hearts, minds, and actions. He wants to distort our worship, thoughts, desires, and actions. Resist. You were meant for so much more than what the

[269] https://castingcrowns.com/music/courageous/

[270] I think they are embarrassed for me or by me for repeating they lyrics so much.

world has to offer. I dare you to start at the cross. I dare you.

5. Doing so will require courage. The United States Marines expect not only physical courage from their men and women, but they also expect moral courage. Marines are expected to lead the charge up the hill, but they are also expected to be courageous enough to stand their moral ground. Christ calls His followers to spiritual courage. Society offers daily opportunities to deny Christ and follow ourselves. In Applied Christianity, students are dared to be more than they were meant to be and to courageously adhere to their professing faith.

   a. One year, a young lady told the class she wanted to lead her family in Christ. Behind her, were her friends who were sneering at the prospect that *she* could do so. No doubt, this young woman would need courage to move her family to where they were meant to be, at the foot of the cross.

More videos on different days
I am Second[271]

(Students watch 10-15 videos)

Week one opens with powerful videos and opportunities to reflect on who we are and where we are going in life. *I am Second* videos provide examples of generally well-known individuals who talk about their lives when their identity and purpose were found in themselves and not in Christ. Despite their relative fame and riches, without Christ, they discovered they were miserable and empty. *I am Second* is a clear profession that Christ's first victory is based on His redemptive work.

Major League Baseball player, Josh Hamilton, leads off the series. Hamilton had everything, until he had nothing. Tragedy took his parents and profession from his life. Like many, Hamilton turned to drugs and alcohol, becoming addicted. Brian 'Head' Welch follows Hamilton's testimony. Welch, once the lead personality of the rock metal group, "Korn," gave up sex, drugs, fame, and fortune to follow Christ. His testimony of God's love is powerful. If Welch can be loved by Christ, anyone can be loved by Christ, struggling high school seniors too.

Other impactful *I am Second* videos shown are:

---

[271] https://www.iamsecond.com/

Tony Dungy: Who you and whose you are in Christ is more important than football.
Chris Plekenpol: I wasn't willing to die for my enemy, but that's exactly what Christ did for me, being an enemy of Him.
Tony Evans: Probably a favorite of mine as he reinforces that our value, identity, and purpose are found in the blood of Christ. On this day, students are reminded that race, ethnicity, and economic status do not preclude us from loving our neighbor. Christians have no choice in who they love. Christ calls us to love as He loves.
Lisa Luby Ryan: Acceptance and identity is found in Christ, not in men, or our failures.
Ashley Rawls: Fighting an eating disorder, Ashley finds comfort in knowing she belongs to the Lord, quoting, Romans 14:7-9, "For none of us lives for ourselves alone, and none of us dies for ourselves alone. If we live, we live for the Lord; and if we die, we die for the Lord. So, whether we live or die, we belong to the Lord. For this very reason, Christ died and returned to life so that he might be the Lord of both the dead and the living."

"In the Words of Satan," The Arrows

Becoming a class favorite, *In the Words of Satan* highlights Satan's seduction. Students watch the video twice, first listening only, followed by taking notes and discussing the lyrics after the second listen. The Arrow's song opens our eyes to how we have been manipulated by the Satan and the world. Astute observers will notice that many of the song's ideas are represented in the 7 questions of a worldview.

Class Reflections:

Satan has been destroying God's creation since the beginning
Satan distorts God's pleasures
He is the liar of liars
Satan views us as puppets who he manipulates
Each person has their own lie that Satan can manipulate
Satan will distort God's truth
According to Satan we are the result of a cosmic explosion
We live not for God, but for ourselves
Meaning is determined by the individual not God
Self-worth is dependent on external standards
Satan uses the media to distort God's plans for His people

Confusion is a primary tool of Satan
Satan uses freedom against Christians

God loves His people, but Satan hides God's love in the pleasures of sin
Christians think we have spirituality, but it is only emotional alchemy

"Be Present", Propaganda

Spoken word artist Propaganda challenges young and old to be present, now.

Class reflections:

1) We cannot hear past the 'explosions' of life, the ones that already happened, or the ones you anticipate:

   a. Students come into the classroom weighed down by the explosions of the past. Perhaps the death of a loved one or a divorce in the family. Maybe they are ashamed of their past and live in the shame, preventing them from enjoying the present.

   b. Anxiety is increasing in today's youth. What college am I going to go to? How will I pay for school? What will I do with the rest of my life? More intense questions may be, why would I invest in a relationship when my last boyfriend or girlfriend abused me? My mother abandoned our family, why should I get married? My aunt lost her child, is having a child even worth it? Past experiences "paralyze" us, and the future "hypnotizes" into anxiety.

2) I can appreciate the excitement seniors have for wanting to graduate. Countdowns to the last day of high school only encourage us to look ahead, missing the moments in front of us. Do not take life for granted, seize the day, and its opportunities.

3) The time we have been given today is where we live. Dwelling in the past weighs us down, looking forward to that which does not even exist only causes more anxiety. Be prudent, but do not freak about what does not exist, the past or the future. You have today, live it well to the glory of God.

"This is Water", David Foster Wallace

Deceased atheist and author, David Foster Wallace's commencement speech at Kenyon College in 2005 has become a viral hit. Foster's speech has been reduced to a nine-minute video titled, "This is Water."

Class reflections:

1) Choose differently. You alone decide how you will respond to any situation at any time.

2) Maintaining a healthy, God-pleasing attitude is your choice. Finding yourself on the end of the bench? Choose how you will respond to the situation. Whining and complaining influences yourself and the team's chemistry, which impacts team success. Instead of complaining, change your perspective. Use your gifts, talents, and abilities to make the team better. Choose differently. Do whatever your current vocation is to God's glory and not with selfish ambition. Do it with integrity, honor, humility, service, and sacrifice. Circumstances may not be ideal or what you (or your parents) expected but stop blaming others and making excuses. Whatever the role and situation, you want to be able to look back at those moments and ask yourself, "Did I do it right?" Do it right.

3) Your perspective influences your decision. In the large scheme of life, does it matter that a driver cut you off on the road? Choosing to be angry at the driver influences your attitude towards not only that person, but possibly you own children. Fuming from the bumper to bumper traffic, you storm into the house yelling at your child because they received a C on a test. Is a low-test grade worth ruining your relationship with your child? What about demeaning children because they missed a wide-open net or basket? Perspective, folks. Some things just don't matter.

4) Students want to hurry up and graduate high school. What awaits graduation? Life. Day in and day out routine. Rush hour traffic. Annoying situations with annoying people. Hurt, pain, fifty weeks of work, day in and day out, for forty years. Why the hurry?

"God's Chisel", The Skit Guys[272]

Shown around homecoming, "God's Chisel" reminds students that Christ has created them anew with His redemptive work on the cross. Shown twice, students are broken into partnerships to discuss what they felt were the most important ideas represented. Students may recall Mr. Horvath standing on a desk declaring, "I am a unique child of God, full of potential, washed in the blood of Christ." Below are a few lines and reflections from the video worthy of reflection.

Class Reflections:

Look into the mirror until you see the work of Christ
You are either moving away from God or towards God
You care too much what others think about you
Fix your eyes on Jesus, the author and perfecter of our faith
Stop going to empty wells that do not offer God's living water
My thoughts are not God's thoughts
My ways are not God's ways
Stop listening to the wrong voices, listen to God's voice
God's name is above all names and is not to be misused
God love us too much to leave us where we are at
God has overcome the world.

How much do you have to hate yourself or friends to leave them where they are at?

God makes us His original masterpiece by His redemptive work on the cross, not by what we do.

---

[272] www.skitguys.com

Appendixes

Appendix 1:

Memorizing Scripture

Scripture encourages the Christian to know and meditate on the Word of God. Deuteronomy 6 instructs the Jews to tie them as symbols on their hands and foreheads. Write the commands on their doorframes so that His commands are always present and within. They are to be mediated on day and night so that "the message of Christ dwell among you richly as you teach and admonish one another with all wisdom through psalms, hymns, and songs from the Spirit, singing to God with gratitude in your hearts."[273]

Memory quizzes happen every Friday in Applied. Instead of asking students to memorize one verse for one week and a new verse the next, we tack verses onto each other. The first week of school, students memorize the class quote and mission statement. The following week, we add Brennan Manning's quote to the previous two. The week after, we add another. After a few weeks of quizzes, students are reciting on paper between four and six memory selections.

When the entire senior class has demonstrated their ability to memorize the first set of verses, we remove the selection from the list, adding a new verse. It sounds terrible, but the process helps the students memorize. Most students find it easier than they expected.

Memory substantially improves cognition.[274] We ask our math students to memorize equations and multiplication tables. What's 3x3? 9. 7x7? 49. We have committed the multiplication tables to memory so that we have a foundation of knowledge to work from and apply later. Why would we deprive our students from memorizing God's Word?

Most of the verses and selections memorized during the school year are provided below. Memory selections always have a direct relationship to the topic being covered in class. My heart jumps for joy when students relate memory into our conversation without instructor guidance.

---

[273] Colossians 3:16

[274] https://www.psychologytoday.com/us/blog/memory-medic/201305/memorization-is-not-dirty-word-2

1st Semester Memory:

Class Quote: I am a unique child of God, full of potential, washed in the blood of Christ.

School Mission Statement: Lutheran North is devoted to academic excellence and above all sharing and modeling the Gospel of Jesus Christ in all aspects of its ministry.

Brennan Manning:
The greatest single cause of atheism in the world today is Christians: who acknowledge Jesus with their lips, walk out the door, and deny Him by their lifestyle. That is what an unbelieving world simply finds unbelievable.

7 Questions of a Worldview:

1. What is prime reality?
2. What is the nature of external reality?
3. What is a human being?
4. What happens to a person at death?
5. Why is it possible to know anything at all?
6. How do we know what is right and wrong?
7. What is the meaning of human history?

Love God, Love People, Share the Gospel

Worldview Definition: A set of presuppositions which we hold about the basic makeup of our world.

River Out of Eden Quote: The universe that we observe has precisely the properties we should expect if there is, at bottom, no design, no purpose, no evil, no good, nothing but pitiless indifference.

Romans 12:2:
Do not conform to the pattern of this world but be transformed by the renewing of your mind. Then you will be able to test and approve what God's will is—his good, pleasing, and perfect will.

1 Peter 3:15:
But in your hearts revere Christ as Lord. Always be prepared to give an answer to everyone who asks you to give the reason for the hope that you have. But do this with gentleness and respect.

Joshua 1:8
Do not let this Book of the Law depart from your mouth; meditate on it day and night, so that you may be careful to do everything written in it. Then you will be prosperous and successful.

139:13-14:
For you created my inmost being you knit me together in my mother's womb. I praise you because I am fearfully and wonderfully made; your works are wonderful; I know that full well.

COSGEEH:

Cellular Organization

1. Order
2. Sensitivity
3. Growth
4. Evolutionary Adaptation
5. Energy Utilization
6. Homeostasis

1 Samuel 16:7
But the Lord said to Samuel, "Do not consider his appearance or his height, for I have rejected him. The Lord does not look at the things people look at. People look at the outward appearance, but the Lord looks at the heart."

Psalm 24:1-2
The earth is the Lord's, and everything in it, the world, and all who live in it; for he founded it on the seas and established it on the waters.

2nd Semester Memory:

Joshua 24:15, But if serving the Lord seems undesirable to you, then choose for yourselves this day whom you will serve, ...But as for me and my household, we will serve the Lord.

Thought Action Steps

1. Recognize
2. Challenge
3. Replace
4. Change behavior

Colossians 2:8
See to it that no one takes you captive through hollow and deceptive philosophy, which depends on human tradition and the elemental spiritual forces of this world rather than on Christ.

Philippians 4:8-9: Finally, brothers and sisters, whatever is true, whatever is noble, whatever is right, whatever is pure, whatever is lovely, whatever is admirable—if anything is excellent or praiseworthy—think about such things. Whatever you have learned or received or heard from me, or seen in me—put it into practice. And the God of peace will be with you.

2 Corinthians 10:5
We demolish arguments and every pretension that sets itself up against the knowledge of God, and we take captive every thought to make it obedient to Christ.

Context quote: A text without a context is a pretext for a proof-text

Three Laws:

1. Law of Cognition
2. Law of Exposure
3. Law of Least Resistance

MEPS (Mental, Emotional, Physical, Spiritual)

2 Peter 1:16
For we did not follow cleverly devised stories when we told you about the coming of our Lord Jesus Christ in power, but we were eyewitnesses of his majesty.

1 Corinthians 15:3, For what I received I passed on to you as of first importance: that Christ died for our sins according to the Scriptures

1 Corinthians 15:4, that he was buried, that he was raised on the third day according to the Scriptures.

1 Corinthians 15:5, and that he appeared to Cephas, and then to the Twelve

1 Corinthians 15:6
After that, he appeared to more than five hundred of the brothers at the same time, most of whom are still living, though some have fallen asleep

1 Corinthians 15:7-8 Then he appeared to James, then to all the apostles, and last of all he appeared to me also, as to one abnormally born.

Genesis 2:24
That is why a man leaves his father and mother and is united to his wife, and they become one flesh.

Appendix 2
Sample Memory Quiz

The box size changes depending on the length of the Scripture verse.

Book:	Chapter:	Verse:	Points Possible:	Awarded:
1 Samuel 16:7			5	

Book:	Chapter:	Verse:	Points Possible:	Awarded:
Brennan Manning Quote			4	

Book:	Chapter:	Verse:	Points Possible:	Awarded:
Romans	12	2	3	

Book:	Chapter:	Verse:	Points Possible:	Awarded:
1 Peter	3	15	2	

Appendix 3
Life Issues Verbal Test Rubric

With a partner, students engage in a conversation with Mr. Horvath on the issues below. Boxes are checked off as the students cover the required content. The students write a practice script out. Rarely do we follow a word for word script because life does not happen that way.

Abortion	**IVF**	**Stem Cell**	**Euthanasia**	**Capital Punishment**	**Stewardship**
Demonstration of *human species*	Process identified- what is it	Idea behind the usage of	Reference to Million Dollar Baby	Genesis 9:6 and its rebuttal of arguments	Definition
Demonstration of human *living with a* property of life	Discussion of embryo being life (built on from abortion)	Differentiation between adult cells and embryonic stem cells	Representation of the major concern with Maggie's attitude	Usage- understanding of Romans 12/13	Scripture Reference
Usage, understanding, response of term *viability*	Concerns Christians have	Explanation as to the concerns Christians have with	*The Screwtape Letter* 21/ownership	Concerned Christian's position on Capital Punishment	Example
Infanticide- logical conclusions of arguments for/against	Method for Christians	Application of World View Question 7	Application of World View Question 7	Usage and understanding of the word moratorium	Concept

Appendix 4
Elements of Thought Chart

This pie chart is used to walk students through the thinking process. Most importantly we want to identify the question and the data and information used to answer the question.

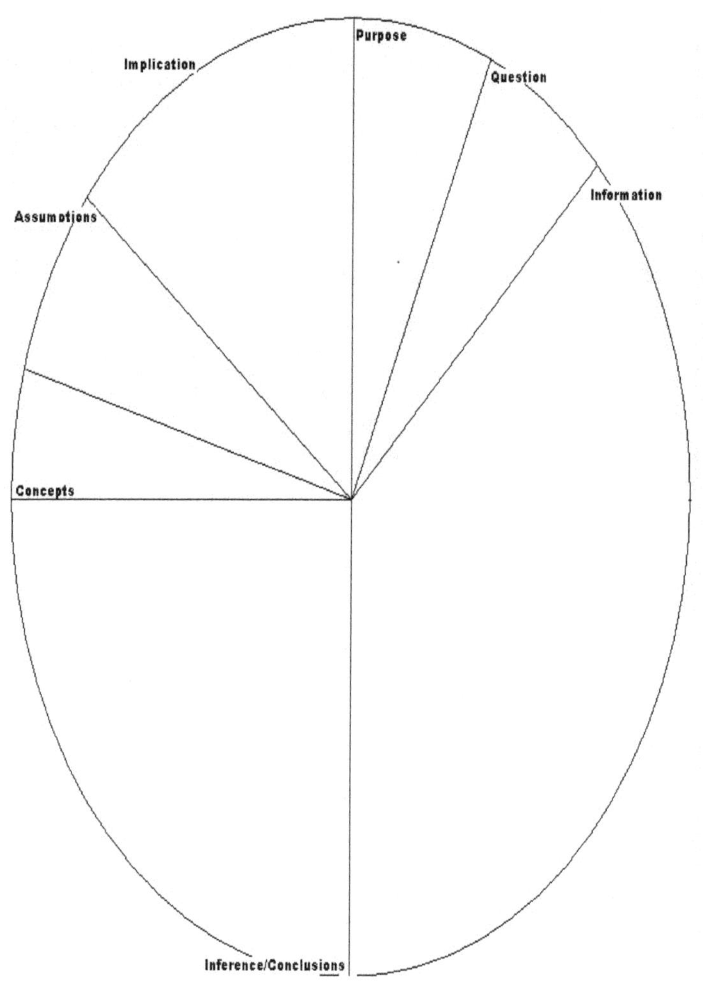

Appendix 5

Change your Life: Think (...on These Things)

Reprinted with permission

Original authors:

Rev. David P. E. Maier
Rev. Bryan Salminen, Ph.D.

Imagine with me, if you will, that you are in fact an Olympic caliber athlete. You are in training for 1,600 and 3,200 meter events at the 2012 Summer Olympics in London, England. With just a little over two years left for training and tryouts, how many of you would begin the Twinkies diet between now and the Games?

As I write this, *The North American International Auto Show* is taking place in Detroit, Michigan. From what I've heard (I've never been there), it's a glitzy display case for the newest in automobile design and technology. If you were fortunate enough to be able to buy one of the display vehicles, would you fill the fuel tank with water, or Gatorade, or your favorite beer?

The food we eat or the fuel we use will ultimately determine the performance and well being of our bodies and our vehicles. Everyone would agree with this. From Atkins Bars or wheatgrass shots to octane boosters and synthetic oils, companies which help us determine what to put into our bodies and into our cars are multi-billion dollar industries.

What could be more important than what we put into our bodies and into our cars? Unfortunately, it is an area that we rarely deliberately consider, or if we do, it is with a "whatever" nonchalance. What you "fuel" your bodies or cars with really pales in comparison with what you feed ... *your minds.*

Paul is speaking to the regenerate child of God in Romans 12:2 about how to live in this world when he writes: "Do not conform any longer to the pattern of this world, but be transformed by the renewing of your mind." In Philippians 4:8and 9 he is even more specific: "Finally, brothers, whatever is true, whatever is noble, whatever is right, whatever is pure, whatever is lovely, whatever is admirable—if anything is excellent or praiseworthy—think about such things. Whatever you have learned or received or heard from me, or seen in me—put it into practice. And the God of peace will be with you." Knowing how to live in this world and doing so with the peace and benediction of our Lord is something we ALL need.

I'd like to share three "laws" with you that I pray will help determine what we will put into our minds and be a huge encouragement to reading the Scriptures on a daily basis. They are: The Law of Cognition, The Law of Exposure, and The Law of Least Resistance.

The Law of Cognition

The Law of Cognition basically says that you are what you think. It is built around the truth that the way you think is the single most important shaper of who you are as a person. The way you think creates your attitudes ... shapes your emotions ... and affects your behavior. (Some would even say that it has a lot to do with your vulnerability to sickness and your immune system.) This basically describes the field of cognitive psychology, one of the most prominent schools in American psychology.

Quite frankly, here's where the social sciences are just beginning to understand what the Holy Spirit made clear to the Scripture writers thousands of years earlier. *Proverbs 23:7*says, *"For as he thinks within himself, so he is."* Jesus stated it in a more comprehensive way in *Matthew 7:17-18, "Likewise every good tree bears good fruit, but a bad tree bears bad fruit. A good tree cannot bear bad fruit, and a bad tree cannot bear good fruit."*

I think one of the things that Jesus is talking about is what goes on inside of us, our thought processes. When our thoughts are healthy, determined, and sound, they will produce a good life. When the thoughts are diseased, unhealthy, destructive, and sinful, they can't bring forth a good life. You are what you think.

The Law of Exposure

The Law of Exposure is this: Whatever your mind is most exposed to, it will think about most. What enters your mind repeatedly occupies your mind, shapes your thoughts, and ultimately expresses itself in what you do and who you become. That's why Paul exhorts: *"Set your minds on things above, not on earthly things," Colossians 3:2.*

Here's a law that no one is surprised about: *the law of gravity*. No one would be taken by surprise if I dropped a crystal wine goblet on our cement garage floor and it shattered. But there remains general surprise over the fact that what our minds are constantly exposed to and dwell upon eventually comes out in how we feel and what we do.

We are flooded by sexual images from screens, terminals, magazine covers, and multiplexes. Then we express astonishment when promiscuity goes up and fidelity goes down and marital stability goes out the door. Our children are exposed to thousands of acts of violence, even graphic violence, on television, in movies, in video "games." Some of these violent acts are even "glorified." Then we express amazement when high school shootings devastate a community like Columbine, Colorado.

Two things need to be remembered:

(1) the mind will absorb and reflect whatever it is exposed to; and

(2) you and I are NOT immune. (No matter how often your children say to you, "I can watch these shows, listen to these lyrics, play these violent games and they don't affect me. I'm not really paying attention..." they're wrong. They are being affected.)

The events you attend, the materials that you read or don't read, the music that you listen to, the images you watch, the conversations that you hold, the daydreams that you entertain, these are shaping your mind, and eventually your character, and ultimately your destiny.

The Law of the Path of Least Resistance

The Law of the Path of Least Resistance states that whatever's easiest is probably the direction of flow. In other words, which is easier: to discipline yourself to exercise or read a book or to turn on the television so that you don't have to take the initiative or be intentional about what is going to fill your mind?

The truth is that many of us are subject to living in an ugly circle where we work continually, are constantly tired, and consequently fall prey to the Law of the Path of Least Resistance. We don't take the time to be still and quiet and make a conscious, determined effort to think about, and put into our minds, *whatever is true, whatever is noble, whatever is right, whatever is pure, whatever is lovely, whatever is admirable ... whatever is excellent or praiseworthy.*

Thinking, the thinking that shapes our lives and behaviors, takes maturity and discipline. Throughout Scripture, God invites us to understand that His blessing in our life comes through time with Him, a relationship with Him, fostered through the reading of His Word. *Psalm 1:1-3: Blessed is the man who does not walk in the counsel of the wicked or stand in the way of sinners or sit in the seat of mockers. But his delight is in the law of the LORD, and on his law he meditates day and night. He is like a tree planted by streams of water, which yields its fruit in season and whose leaf does not wither. Whatever he does prospers.*

Here, then, is where the Law of Exposure works positively in our behalf. If we really want to become a different kind of person – one that is true, noble, right, pure, lovely admirable, excellent and praiseworthy – it really is possible through the forgiveness and strength that Christ offers; it's possible as we meet Him in the reading and studying of His inspired, holy Word. There, in the study of His Word, is the best place to be confronted by, and to start thinking, different thoughts.

This will not happen automatically, but Scripture indicates a few things we can do:

First, monitor your mind. In fact the Apostle Paul says that we should "take captive every thought to make it obedient to Christ," 2 Corinthians 10:5.

Second, we need to heed the Law of Exposure: that is, we need to expose our minds to those resources—books, tapes, people, conversations—that will incline our minds to embrace the right kinds of subjects and thoughts. This will help protect us from the wrong kinds of damaging influences, because every source will move our minds one way or another.

Third, begin by doing something radical like shutting the TV off for a week, limiting your iPod time, or even your computer time. Your mind may need that just to create space for other thoughts. What I especially want to encourage you to do is this: make a commitment to say, "I will increasingly expose my mind to God's Word through a daily study of Scripture."

Friends, God has given us this Word for the transformation of our minds. He has given us this Word, in part, so that we can think about what's true and honorable and pure and good and wholesome. Please make the effort. Part of this involves a corporate activity where we come together on a weekly basis for worship and Bible Study or Small Group Bible Study.

But, then there's a real personal, private part. The Bible talks a lot about the idea of meditating on Scripture. In the very first Psalm it says that the man of God meditates on Scripture day and night. It just becomes a habitual thing.

Now the word *"meditate,"* I know, can be a little scary for some. So let me make it as simple as possible: How many of you know how to worry? If you know how to worry, you know how to meditate. Think of meditation as a positive form of worry. You take one thought, and you dwell on it and linger on it and absorb it until it becomes a part of you. You meditate on Scripture and, in this process, another beneficial choice would be to actually memorize Scripture.

The psalmist talks about memorization and its benefits: *"I have hidden your Word in my heart that I might not sin against You," Psalm 119:11*. It really does not matter how many verses you stow away. It's not a quantity deal; however, in the act of saying, rehearsing, reflecting on, and absorbing Scripture, your mind changes. That thought from God's Word becomes a part of your mind. It becomes a kind of filter or screen. It becomes something that's excellent and praiseworthy that's in you and that becomes a part of you. You begin to live on the basis of that Word.

I pray that reading and studying the Word of God becomes a part of your daily life that you anticipate and cherish. Through the work of the Holy Spirit in the Word may our lives be continually transformed as our minds are filled with excellent, admirable, honorable, and praiseworthy thoughts.

And as good and beneficial as that will be, remember: "No eye has seen, no ear has heard, no mind has conceived what God has prepared for those who love Him," 1 Corinthians 2:9.

www.ingramcontent.com/pod-product-compliance
Lightning Source LLC
Chambersburg PA
CBHW030633150426
42811CB00048B/64

* 9 7 8 0 5 7 8 6 8 3 0 9 6 *